Pigsfoot Jelly
&
Persimmon Beer

PIGSFOOT JELLY & PERSIMMON BEER

Foodways from the Virginia Writers' Project

Edited by Charles L. Perdue, Jr.

Ancient City Press
Santa Fe, New Mexico

International Standard Book Number: 0-941270-74-2

Library of Congress Catalogue Number: 92-09356

First Edition

Designed by Mary Powell

Cover design by Connie Duran

Cover photograph: Nicholson Hollow in the Shenandoah National Park Area, Virginia. October 1935. John [T.] Nicholson peeling apples. Photography by Arthur Rothstein.

Frontispiece: A Little Negro Girl Helping to Serve the Food. Camp Pleasant, Virginia. August 1941. U.S. Department of Agriculture Photographer William J. Forsythe. [N-2174]. [Camp Pleasant was located at Chopawomsic—later Prince William Forest Park—an early Resettlement Administration project. One thousand under-privileged children from the District of Columbia spent the summer at the Camp, learning various craft, recreational, and other skills.]

Library of Congress Cataloging-in-Publication Data

Pig's foot jelly and persimmon beer : foodways from the Virginia Writers' Project /
   compiled and edited by Charles L. Perdue, Jr. — 1st ed.
      p.   cm.
   Includes bibliographical references.
   ISBN 0-941270-74-2 :
   1. Food habits—Virginia—History. 2. Cookery—Virginia. 3. Cookery, American—
Southern style. 4. Virginia—Social life and customs. I. Perdue, Charles L., 1930-   .
II. Virginia Writers' Project.
GT2853.U54P54 1992
394.1'09755—dc20   92-9356
                                                                             CIP

10   9   8   7   6   5   4   3   2   1

Contents

Preface

This book is one of a number of publications derived from the work of the New Deal cultural programs in Virginia which my wife, Nancy J. Martin-Perdue, and I began researching in 1969—when we first began to look for the ex-slave interviews made in Virginia by workers of the Virginia Writers' Project.[1]

The intention is to make generally available Virginia cultural resources that, but for the intervention of World War II, would have been available some fifty years ago. By so doing, we wish to emphasize the rich traditional heritage of Virginia and Virginians and also to give credit to the workers who helped to preserve this material and to the people from whom it came.

A portion of the research for this work was done under a grant awarded jointly to my wife and me by the National Endowment for the Humanities and we are grateful for that agency's support. I wish to acknowledge the assistance of the staff of the Manuscripts Division, and Prints and Photographs Division, Library of Congress; and I express my appreciation to Mikell Brown and Mark Scala of the Pictures Collection, Virginia State Library and to the staff of the Archives Branch, Virginia State Library; to Michael F. Plunkett and the staff of Manuscripts Department, Division of Special Collections, Alderman Library, University of Virginia, Charlottesville; and to Fritz Malval, Archivist at Hampton University. And I want to here thank Nancy J. Martin-Perdue for her reading of the manuscript and subsequent helpful suggestions.

General Abbreviations

FSA   Farm Security Administration

FWP   Federal Writers' Project

VHI   Virginia Historic Inventory Project

VWP   Virginia Writers' Project. Technically, between its establishment in October 1935 and July 1939, one should refer to the Virginia office of the Federal Writers' Project; between July 1939 and the demise of the project in June 1942 it is correct to refer to the Virginia Writers' Project. For convenience sake I will use VWP to cover the entire period of 1935-1942.

WPA   Works Progress Administration (1935-39); Work Projects Administration (1939-43)

Abbreviations: Depositories and Sources

HU/REL   Roscoe E. Lewis Papers, Archives, Hampton University, Hampton, Virginia

LC/AE   Library of Congress, Manuscripts Division, WPA Box A833, Special Studies and Projects, Folder, "America Eats" (Va.).

LCP&P   Library of Congress, Prints and Photographs Division.

UVA/FC   WPA Folklore Collection (Accession No. 1547), Manuscripts Division, Special Collections Department, Alderman Library, University of Virginia, Charlottesville. For an inventory of the material contained in this collection see citation in end note #1.

VSA   WPA-FWP Boxes 178-191, Archives Branch, Virginia State Library, Richmond.

VSL/PC   Picture Collections, Reference & Collection, Virginia State Library, Richmond.

Editorial Procedures

The texts included here are presented in their entirety with these exceptions: I have occasionally modified punctuation in cases where confusion seemed possible; rarely I have changed a word for purposes of clarity and readability; and I have added a gloss in brackets where I thought a term might not be understood.

1. Se e Charles L. Perdue, Jr., Thomas E. Barden, and Robert K. Phillips. *Weevils in the Wheat: Interviews with Virginia Ex-Slaves*. Charlottesville: University Press of Virginia, 1976 (paperback edition Bloomington: Indiana University Press, 1980) [*Weevils* went out of print at Indiana in February 1991 but will be available in paperback from the University Press of Virginia in 1992]; Perdue, et al. *An Annotated Listing of Folklore Collected by Workers of the Virginia Writers' Project, Work Projects Administration—Held in the Manuscripts Department at Alderman Library of the University of Virginia*. Philadelphia: Norwood Editions, 1979; Charles L. Perdue, Jr., ed. *Outwitting the Devil: Jack Tales from Wise County, Virginia*. Santa Fe, NM: Ancient City Press, 1987; Nancy J. Martin-Perdue and Charles L. Perdue, Jr. *Talk About Trouble: A New Deal Portrait of Virginians in the Great Depression*. Chapel Hill: University of North Carolina Press, in press; and Charles L. Perdue, Jr., and Nancy J. Martin-Perdue. *"A Higher Form of Hypocrisy": The New Deal and the Shaping of Culture in Virginia*, in preparation.

Introduction

THE FEDERAL WRITERS' PROJECT [FWP], along with similar projects for Art, Music, and Theatre, was established in August 1935 for purposes of providing some relief to white collar and professional workers. The initial task of the FWP was to produce a series of state guidebooks modeled somewhat on the style of the Baedeker guidebooks of Western Europe. At the beginning there was concern that the FWP might not last long enough to complete the work for the guides but, as the Great Depression wore on the Writers' Project did continue, and, as the guidebooks neared completion, additional projects were begun— both while the Writers' Project was under Federal control (27 July 1935-31 August 1939) and under state control (1 September 1939-30 June 1942).[1]

One of the projects begun, but never completed, was work on a book to be called *America Eats*. As originally conceived the book was to consist of:

> A general introduction on development of American cookery [and] five sections covering the country by regions. Each section to consist of an essay on the development of cookery within the region and on the numerous social gatherings at which eating is an important part of the program, with emphasis on dishes and methods of cooking characteristic of the locality; detailed description of two to four gatherings characteristic of the region.[2]

Although there are some references to the idea of a national book on food as early as 1938—possibly in connection with the gathering of information on foods for the publication U.S. One: Maine to Florida:

Serious discussion of the America Eats project appears to
have begun in August of 1941, when Lyle Saxon, a well-
known and respected member of the Louisiana Writers' Project was formally approached as the prospective national
editor for the publication.[3]

Saxon was also to be the regional editor for the South, which included
Virginia.

The first general announcement of the America Eats project in
Virginia was sent to VWP workers on 13 October 1941:

Dear Fellow-Worker:

Mrs. Katharine Kellock of the Writers' Program in
Washington is working on a book that will be entitled *America
Eats*. I am contributing a chapter on a Virginia family reunion
and the foods served on such an occasion. Now Mrs. Kellock
has requested me to ask our workers to submit stories of some
typical festivities, emphasizing Virginia foods. These sketches
should not exceed 500 words—less than two pages of
typewritten copy.

Take any subject that seems to you interesting—a church
supper, a fish fry, an oyster roast, a Christmas open house, a
box supper, a protracted meeting dinner, a hunters' dinner, or
something of the kind. Get into your story some characteriza-
tion of the people, as well as the appearance and the odor of
the foods.

I want to send all the stories to Mrs. Kellock for embodi-
ment in the introduction to the section entitled "The South
Eats." The manuscripts must be in Washington by October
19.

Sincerely yours,
(signed) Eudora Ramsay Richardson[4]

An undated page (probably by Katharine Kellock) lists prospective
topics for Virginia:

Seafood Dinner on the Eastern Shore
Old Fashioned Brunswick Stew & Barbecue
Oyster Roast in Tidewater Virginia
Old Virginia Breakfast
And continues:

*View of Smithfield (Isle of Wight County), Virginia. WPA
Photographer W. Lincoln Highton. Virginia State Library and
Archives. [A9-7484].*

> We believe the family reunion would be the best subject for
> detailed treatment by Virginia. We would also like to have a
> good recipe for mint julep with some discussion of the various
> conflicting theories concerning its preparation. Also any
> historical information possible on the julep. An account of the
> Christmas eggnog party will also be welcome, as well as infor-
> mation about Brunswick Stew.[5]

In addition to the sketches described by Richardson's letter, the
"regional editors were requested to obtain from each state an annotated
bibliography of cookbooks which featured foods typical of, or peculiar
to, the state."[6]

The results of the national call for food essays was uneven. Some state
directors responded only reluctantly, others enthusiastically. Thirty-
seven states sent in essays to the Washington office; Nebraska sent thirty-
four, Colorado sent twenty-seven, Iowa sent twenty-six, and Virginia sent
twenty. The remaining states sent fewer essays; several states—Con-
necticut, Idaho, Maryland, New Hampshire, New Jersey, and Utah—
sent only one essay.[7] The sparse material from some states resulted
from increasing pressures from the war effort; many staff writers had
to be reassigned to other projects more appropriate to that effort.

Ultimately, *America Eats* succumbed to the war effort. Editorial work
on the manuscript was abruptly terminated in February 1942—along
with other projects. The material sent in for the project languished in
a Library of Congress warehouse in Alexandria, Virginia until 1975.
It is now housed in the Library's Manuscripts Division.[8]

Food is, of course, not simply nourishment; it is also cultural symbol.
The issue of just which foods are "proper" to eat and how one should
prepare them is a subject with the power to stir up considerable excitement.[9] The following exchange of letters between Eudora Ramsay
Richardson, State Director of the VWP and Henry G. Alsberg, Director of the FWP is only partly tongue-in-cheek. The subject was information on Virginia foods to be used in the forthcoming book, *U.S. One:
Maine to Florida.*[10]

*Smithfield Hams in a Smokehouse. Virginia State Library and Archives.
[4701].*

Richardson to Alsberg (17 March 1938):

After all the pains I took to set you Yankees straight concerning orthodox Virginia foods, I am now in quite a state!

Yellow cornmeal can't even be bought South of the Mason and Dixon Line. It may be fed to hogs, but we certainly do not serve it on our tables.

Your receipt for Brunswick Stew is an amazing thing. Never would the most heretical cook put *okra, carrots,* and *celery* into our delectable concoction. I sent in the facts—based upon careful research.

What New York chef told your editors how to prepare Smithfield Ham? I tremble to think what the natives of Smithfield will say when they hear that the ham should be *slashed* and prepared with a paste made of brown sugar and sherry, dotted with cloves, and covered with cracker crumbs. You will note in my manuscript dealing with Virginia Foods, sent to you August 16, 1937, that I put the following footnote, "Southside Virginia considers no heresy more heinous than belief that old hams should be coated with brown sugar and pierced by myriads of cloves." I am already receiving telephone calls from outraged Virginians who are distressed to see their culinary art so misrepresented. It is small comfort to refer to my original manuscript and see that a Virginian told you the truth and that some Yankee distorted the story.

Alsberg to Richardson (19 March 1938):

Your letter on the Virginia food list in *U.S. One* puts us in a dilemma. The insertion of the word "yellow" before corn meal is probably a Yankee slip, but the origin of the recipes for Brunswick Stew and baked ham is echt [genuine] Virginian. We did not realize that two Virginians did not always agree on recipes.

The two recipes to which you object so violently came to this office in the handwriting of Mrs. James Southall Wilson. When we were preparing the list of foods last August Mrs. Wilson offered these two recipes and knowing her reputation as a cook we accepted the courtesy.

Perhaps it would be well to start a contest with examples. This office is quite willing to sacrifice digestion to the cause. I am very sorry that we did not submit these recipes to you before we sent them to press.

Richardson to Alsberg (29 March 1938):

I have mailed this morning to you—attention of Mrs. Kellock—a package containing Smithfield ham and beaten biscuits. I shall have to admit that I did not make the biscuits. I did cook the ham, however, according to accepted Virginia standards, untouched by Northern influences.

Until Mrs. James Southall Wilson sends you a sample of her culinary art, will you please withhold judgment? The next time I come to Washington I expect to arrive, carrying in one hand a pail filled with Brunswick Stew and in the other, cornbread that hasn't the slightest golden tinge.

Katharine A. Kellock to Richardson (30 March 1938):

I write for all members of the staff who had the pleasure of sampling the Virginia ham—and biscuits. We are convinced. I can only say this is the most satisfactory form of criticism we have ever received. Mr. Alsberg, in the middle of a conference, took a piece of ham in one hand and a couple of beaten biscuits in the other and went on with business.

I have included in this work the twenty America Eats manuscripts that Virginia sent to the Washington office of the FWP and that are listed in J. Charles Camp's checklist (see endnote #2) as well as two other manuscripts found in the same file but not indicated by Camp. These twenty-two items are indicated in an endnote to each as "Loc. LC/AE." With the exception of one piece by Susan R. Morton and two by Essie W. Smith, these items intended for the America Eats book were written by office researchers and writers.

I have added to this basic material all of the items on food and foodways found in the folklore collection made by field workers of the VWP. For these, I have indicated "Loc. UVA/FC." These field collected materials provide an interesting complement to the essays.

Finally, so that the book will have a larger perspective, I have added information on slave foods from the Virginia ex-slave interviews previously published by Perdue, et al. I believe that, over all, and within the time frame covered, the material presented provides a comprehensive view of Virginians at the table.

Notes

1. The first public announcement of the establishment of these arts projects (designated Federal No. 1) was on 2 August 1935 but it was October by the time they had received final Presidential approval, been funded, and procedural instructions sent to the field. For Virginia's guide, see *Virginia: A Guide to the Old Dominion.* Compiled by workers of the Writers' Program of the Work Projects Administration in the State of Virginia. New York: Oxford University Press, 1940. For an in-depth discussion of the various projects and programs with which the Virginia Writers' Project was involved, see Charles L. Perdue, Jr., and Nancy J. Martin-Perdue. *A Higher Form of Hypocrisy,* ibid.

2. Quoted in J. Charles Camp. "America Eats: Toward a Social Definition of American Foodways." Ph.D. dissertation, University of Pennsylvania, 1978, p. 96. Camp provides a thorough discussion of the America Eats project, complete with a checklist of manuscript material sent to the Washington office of the Writers' Project. Camp states that he "failed to turn up a single reference to the America Eats project," in the Archives Branch of the Virginia State Library in Richmond, but, in fact, this material had been deposited instead in Alderman Library, University of Virginia. One suspects that there is more information to be found in other state depositories that would fill in some of the "significant gaps" that Camp finds in the historical record.

3. Camp, "America Eats," ibid, p. 92.

4. Loc. UVA/FC.

5. Loc. LC/AE.

6. Camp, "America Eats," p. 104.

7. Camp, "America Eats," ibid, from checklist in Chapter two.

8. Camp, "America Eats," ibid, p. 91.

9. An analysis of cultural foodways is beyond the scope of this particular work but the reader might consult the following: Linda Keller Brown and Kay Mussell. *Ethnic and Regional Foodways in the United States: The Performance of Group Identity.* Knoxville: University of Tennessee Press, 1984; Charles Camp. *American Foodways: What, When, Why and How We Eat in America.* Little Rock, AR: August House, 1990; Michael Owen Jones, Bruce Giuliano, and Roberta Krell. *Foodways & Eating Habits: Directions for Research.* Los Angeles: California Folklore Society, 1983. Theodore C. Humphrey and Lin T. Humphrey. eds. *"We Gather Together": Food and Festival in American Life.* Ann Arbor, MI: UMI Research Press, 1988.

10. Loc. UVA/FC.

The Texts

VIRGINIA EATS

[ED. NOTE: The first item included here is, appropriately enough, what are likely the earliest comments on foodways in Virginia— those made by Capt. John Smith in the first year of settlement of Jamestown.][1]

1607: "This place I call *mulbery shade*. He caused heere to be prepared for us *pegatewk-Apyan* which is bread of their wheat made in Rolles and Cakes; this the weomen make, and are very clenly about it; we had parched meale, excellent good; . . . " [Capt. Gabriel Archer]. *(Pt. I, p. xlviii).*

1607: " . . . and ere long more bread and venison was brought him then would have served twentie men." *(Pt. II, p. 397).*

1607: "*Opitchapam* the Kings brother invited him to his house, where, with as many platters of bread, foule, and wild beasts, as did environ him, he bid him wellcome; . . . " *(Ibid, p. 399).*

1607: " . . . more than fortie platters of fine bread stood as a guard in two fyles on each side the doore." *(Pt. II, p. 405).*

1607: "I [George Percy] saw Bread made by their women, which doe all their drugerie. . . . The manner of baking of bread is thus. After they pound their wheat into flowre, with hote water they make it into paste, and worke it into round balls and Cakes; then they put it into a pot of seething water; when it is sod thoroughly, they lay it on a smooth stone, there they harden it as well as in an Oven." *(Pt. I, p. lxix).*

May 26, 1607: "This night we went some—mile, and ankored at a place I call *kynd womans care* which is—mile from *Mulbery shade*. Here we came within night, yet was there ready for us of bread new made, sodden wheate and beans, mullberyes, and some fishe undressed more then all we could eate. Moreover thes people seemed not to crave any thing in requitall, Howbeit our Captain voluntarily distributed guifts." [Captain Gabriel Archer]. *(Pt. I, p. xlix).*

1607: " . . . the meanest sort brought us such dainties as they had, and of their bread which they make of their Maiz[e] or Gennea wheat. They would not suffer us to eat unless we sate down, which we did on a mat right against them." [George Percy]. *(Pt. I, p. lxiii).*

1607: " . . . His people gave us mullberyes, sodd wheate and beanes, and he [their king] caused his weomen to make Cakes for us . . . " [Capt. Gabriel Archer]. *(Pt. I, p. xliii).*[2]

NEW ENGLANDER'S INITIATION TO VIRGINIA COOKING

COOKING—THIS IS A TRUISM—must be judged by the results. Preliminary, of course, is temptation. This may be analyzed into name-suggestion, appearance, atmosphere, including odors, and—what you have?

For years the French have been credited with artistry in cooking. But conning over memories of American cooking, one wonders whether Virginians—those of the Old Dominion and their cousins from New England, have not also achieved a high standard in what constitutes excellent food.

The modern home, with all its new-fangled contraptions, has merely elaborated the kitchen. The traditions have been preserved.

The New England kitchen—this from an adopted Virginian—in association with which I was introduced to all that originated at the cook-stove, was the home's living room. Mother was the cook. The "hired girl" was a daughter of a poor but respectable family, who had come to live with us, "earn her board and keep."

When my sister married a Virginian, she brought to her new home the traditions of expertness under which she had been reared. Accessory to her supervision—Virginia style—she not unlikely put on a big apron, rolled up her sleeves, and proceeded to demonstrate to Emma, the colored help, the manner in which she (sister) had been taught to do things.

Sister's kitchen, then, was an institution; a "shop" where food was prepared expertly. Doubtless Emma learned from her many things about cooking. I am sure that Sister learned from her. For once, when the "young bride" had sent home from the market where she had chosen it, a naked fowl of uncertain age, whose body resembled that of a well-trained athlete, Emma—so it is related—said nothing, but proceeded to boil—or whatever cooks do under such circumstances—the ancient biddie, and for final preparations produced a foundation that developed into a really palatable dish.

With such a background—as a guest—I received my introduction to Virginia cooking. Years later, and at long last, having made intimate contact with what folk call "Southern cooking," I visited Sister's home, now supervised by a charming niece. The now white-haired Emma still presided in the kitchen. And when the fried chicken with gravy, toast browned to the last proper turn, "batter bread," corn pudding, "greens," had been disposed of, I was not surprised, as satisfied, having edged back my chair a little from the table, to see Emma bringing in dessert.

I had eaten well, if sparingly, and relaxed with the comfortable "full feeling" that follows—or ought to follow—all good meals, guided, of course by knowledge that years, if they had not tampered materially with my digestion, had at least deprived it of youthful zest.

Emma appeared, I say, with a huge cake, and closely followed by her younger assistant with ice cream.

I recalled, then, mother's plan, decades before, for restraining the often too eager appetites of her youngsters. She promised more dessert—usually pie—if we would eat more meat and vegetables.

So, if I tasted only meagerly, as one does under such circumstances, it was not because traditions were lacking, but out of my knowledge that years had decreed watchfulness for the inner man.

Everything, apparently, was there: temptation, atmosphere—social and odorful—and artistry. One does not analyze happiness. One does not analyze cooking but by the result. I cannot tell how those things were prepared. I know only that this feast—for "feast" it was—carried with it all the earmarks of excellence, the combined supervision, the traditions—Old Virginia and New England—of the "old home," that may have reached backward into the foundations of Anglo-Saxon good living.[3]

∽ ∾

COOKING IN GRAND-MOTHER'S AND GREAT GRAND-MOTHER'S DAY

THEY COOKED THE same as all did in the old plantation days, by the fireplace. They say that they cooked fine pies and cakes and also corn-pone, in the large iron spiders that they used in those days for fire-place cooking. They had legs so coals could be raked under them, and they were covered over tight with iron lids, so they would retain the heat; anything that should be cooked quickly or required more heat, coals were also put on top the lids.

In baking cake—that had to be baked slowly—the spiders were well lined with paper. The favorites were pound cakes, both sugar and molasses pound cakes. They used the same recipe that is generally used to-day, which has been handed down from generation to generation to the present day.

The sugar pound cakes were made as follows:

> *One pound of sugar*
> *One pound of butter*
> *From 9 to 12 eggs*
> *One pound of flour*
> *Mix cake with milk*
> *And flavor with lemon.*

The molasses pound cake was made the same, only molasses was used instead of sugar, and spices were used in place of lemon for flavoring.[4]

∽ ∾

NEGRO PLANTATION LIFE: COOKING BY THE FIREPLACE

ALL THE COOKING was done in the fireplace: For baking or roasting they had huge iron ovens, with heavy covers; they were first heated in the fire then they were placed as near the fire as it would require to keep them at the right temperature; then the food was put in and covered over, a few live coals were raked up around the oven, also a few coals were placed on top. In these ovens they baked whole hams, turkeys, and even little pigs.

For cornpone or other foods that required less space, they used iron spiders, they had legs, and heavy covers. They used a sort of iron paddle with a long handle for lifting the covers from the ovens and spiders.

Waffles were also cooked in the fireplace: The waffle irons had long iron handles. And there was quite an art in cooking waffles in the fireplace, to keep them from burning.

For boiling, or stewing, they used iron kettles, which were swung on a crane. Water was also boiled by placing a kettle on the crane.

At an earlier period, roasting was done on a spit. A spit, was a long iron rod with a knob on one end to turn it with. This rod was run through the andirons, which were real tall, and were made with openings in the top for the spit to run through.

On the spit they cooked turkeys, geese and other fowl, also game. They even roasted whole pigs. This was done by putting the spit through whatever was to be roasted. A large iron pan was placed under the spit to catch the drippings. As the food roasted, from time to time, the knob on the end of the spit was turned to prevent burning of the food, and to brown it evenly.

One of the most difficult and trying articles of food to cook in the fireplace was coffee, for all the coffee was bought in the unroasted bean state, and the roasting of it was quite a task; it was roasted in the iron spiders with covers. The difficulty was in roasting it without burning.

Hominy Making: Hominy making was done by the slaves. First, the corn was soaked over night in weak lye water, to soften and loosen the skin. In the morning it was put in the mortar; then the pestle, which was a sort of iron mallet with a long handle, was heated until real hot; then the corn was beaten to remove the skin and crack the corn; it was then put in vats of water, so the loosened skin would rise to the surface; then they would skim it off. It was then taken from the vat and spread out to dry, then it was ready for use.[5]

∽ ∾

RECIPES FROM GLOUCESTER COURT HOUSE AND NEAR BY COMMUNITIES

Boiled Indian Pudding: Mix one quart of corn meal with 3 quarts of milk; take care it be not lumpy—add 3 eggs and a gill [one-fourth pint] of molasses; it must be put on at sunrise, to eat at three o'clock; the great art in this pudding is tying the bag properly, as the meal swells very much.

Pumpkin Pudding: Stew a fine sweet pumpkin till soft and dry; rub it through a sieve; add to the pulp six eggs beaten quite light, a¼ lb. of butter, a½ pint of new milk, some pounded ginger and nutmeg, a wine glass of brandy, and sugar to your taste. Should it be too liquid, stew it a little drier; put a paste round the edges and in the bottom of a shallow dish or plate—pour in the mixture, cut some thin bits of paste, twist them and put them across the top and bake it nicely.

Vinegar of the Four Thieves: Take lavender, rosemary, sage, worm-wood, rue, and mint, of each a large handfull: Put them in a earthen ware pot, pour on them 4 quarts of very strong vinegar, cover the pot closely, and put a board on the top; keep it in the hottest sun two weeks, then strain and bottle it, putting in each bottle a clove of garlic. When it has settled in the bottle, and becomes clear, pour it off gently; do this until you get it all free from sediment. The proper time to make it is when the herbs are in full vigor in June. This vinegar is very refreshing in crowded rooms, and in the rooms of the sick; and it is peculiarly grateful about the house in damp weather.

Bread Pudding Recipe:
>   *1 cup of sugar*
>   *2 cups of milk*
>   *2 tablespoonfuls of butter*
>   *4 level teaspoonfuls of baking powder*
>   *2 eggs, well beaten*
>   *1 qt. of flour, or enough to make a stiff batter*
>   *1 teaspoonful of salt*
>   *2 cups of raisins*

Turn pudding into a muslin bag and put into a kettle of boiling water, be sure that there is enough water to cover it; keep it boiling briskly for one hour and a half; and be careful that the water does not stop boiling 'till the pudding is done, or it will be heavy. It should be eaten while hot, with hard sauce, or any kind of liquid sauce that is preferred.

Making Yeast: In olden times, as they had no yeast, in Gloucester it is said that they raised some kind of plant from seed, which was called yeast plant, and from that they made yeast; after they made the yeast they let it ferment, then it was ready to use. They say that they made good light bread and rolls with it, and anything else that required yeast to raise it.[6]

∽ ∾

FOOD AND DRINKS OF VIRGINIA

THE KITCHEN WAS filled with assistants famed for their special skill in particular branches of the art of cookery. They bustled about with glistening faces and shining teeth, proud of their elevation and eager to add to the general cheer.

It is impossible to describe the famed dinner, for love, happiness, hospitality, and general good cheer were a part of it.

The old mahogany table, stretched diagonally across the dining room, groaned; the big gobbler filled the place of honor; a great round of beef held the second place; and old ham and every other dish that ingenuity, backed by long experience, could devise, was at the side and the shining sideboard, gleaming with glass, scarcely held the dessert.

The butler and his assistants were supernaturally slow, which bespoke plainly too frequent a recourse to the apple toddy bowl; but, under stimulus of the mistress's eye, they got through alright, and their slight unsteadiness was overlooked.

After dinner there was apple toddy and egg-nog, as there had been before. There was also games and dances—country dances, the lancers and quadrills, and the never-to-be forgotten Virginia reel.[7]

∽ ∾

LEATHER BREECHES

THESE BEAUTIFUL FALL days have certainly been an inspiration for one to get out in the country and see the beauties of nature.

Most of the people are gathering in their fruits and vegetables for the winter, making sorghum molasses and stringing red peppers.

Two ladies were stringing green beans. They would snap the ends off and pull the strings off, then with a needle and thread make long strings of them and hang them up behind the stove, she said she let them hang there until they dried and then cook them as any other beans. She called them *Leather Breeches.*[8]

ᴓ ᴕ

SHUCKIE BEANS

BACK FORTY, FIFTY, sixty years ago when I was a girl an' young woman ever'body had shuckie beans. Some people has 'em yit. I usually dry me a few ever' fall. But most people call 'em jes plain dried beans now, an' I've heard somebody call 'em fodder beans. But when I was young ever'body called 'em shuckie beans. They'uz good, too, I'm a tellin' you! A whole lot better, I think, than any o' yo' can beans like they are puttin' up this day an' time.

The way they'd fix 'em was to pick, oh, several bushels o' beans of a day an' then that night they'd most time have a bean stringin' an' all the neighbors'ud come in an' help string em an' thread em' on long pieces o' twine or jes plain sewin' thread. Most times they'd git twine, 'f they could. Hit was stronger. 'F they couldn't git twine then they'd use jes plain sewin' thread an' double hit. They all tell tales while they'uz stringing the beans, an' aiter they got done the children would play games like blindfold, an' the old folks would set 'round an' watch 'em an' tell more tales, an' riddles.

The long strings o' shuckie beans would be hung up against the wall, an' nearly ever' woman in the neighborhood 'ud try an' see 'f she couldn't have more shuckie beans than anybody else. An' they'd show their shuckie beans to one another jes like they did their stack o' quilts.

The way they cooked 'em was to jes take down a string o' the beans an' throw it in a kittle of watter an' let hit cook till the beans'uz tender. Then they'd shift 'em. That is they take 'em out o' the kittle an' pour the water out, wash the pot, an' pull all the beans off o' the threads an' break 'em up in little pieces an' put 'em back in the kittle an' put a big chunk o' fat meat in with 'em. Here lately they've got to breakin' 'em up an' lookin' 'em (removing any foreign matter—JTA) before they put 'em on to cook an' puttin' the meat in right then a' not shiftin' 'em a-tall. They wash 'em in cold water now before they cook 'em.

The biggest trouble with shuckie beans the way they used to do 'em was gittin' hairs in 'em. They jes hung thar against the wall an' you know they'uz liable to catch a lot o' stray hairs.

That made me think of it. I used to hear 'em sing a song about shuckie bean. Ol' Uncle Denton Gibson's folks'uz said to be nasty. An' from what I heard said they wasn't any too clean about their cookin'. One time Lewis Adkins, Letch Collins an' some other fellers was runnin' a thrashin' machine an' they was at ol' Uncle Denton's, thrashin' an' they told the awfulist tales you ever heard in your life aiter they left thar.

Well, sir, Letch Collins he was sort o' funny feller. Allus goin' on with some foolishness. An' he made up a song 'bout what happened to the thrashin' crew at old Uncle Denton's. Hit had some nasty words in it. I wouldn't sing it a-tall. But I don't reckon hit'ud be any sin jes to tell you how one verse went. Hit tol' about 'em settin' down to eat an' what they all seed. They'uz more'n this, but I don't recolect any more o' it. The verse I remember was:

> *Hair in the sallet;*
> *Cat tird in the beans;*
> *Louse in the buttermilk*
> *Lewis Adkins seen.*

I remember hearin' Letch tell it. An' he'd jes rare back an' nearly kill hisse'f laughin'. Said that he went to take out some shuckie beans an' thar was a great big piece o' cat manure in 'em. An' Letch said that Lewis Adkins said he reached out an' got his glass o' buttermilk an' started to take a sup an' thar on top o' the milk, swimmin' right torge him was the biggest ol' head louse he ever seed in his life. So that's what made Letch make the song up.[9]

∽ ∾

HOW SALT WAS MADE

BACK IN THE OLD days when salt was scarce the people used to take the salt water from the Chesapeake Bay and boil it in large kettles. They also used a large copper dipper and as the water evaporated the dipper was sided to dip out the salt. If salt was made in large quantities it was sold to the people near by and they were always glad to get it, as there were no salt mines near and salt was hard to get.

On one occasion while making salt, something happened to the solution and instead of the regular salt that had always been made, a substance like salt, but with a bitter taste, was extracted. Upon examination the doctors said it was salts and arranged to buy all that they made from then on.[10]

∽ ∾

"MAKIN' OUT" IN WAR TIMES

A BROWN DYE WAS made from the root of wild plum. . . the back of the root boiled and copperas added. Another shade of brown was made in the same manner but the bark of walnut was used. Yellow dye was made from broomsage.

A baking soda substitute was made from ashes of hard maple and corn cobs.

Bread was made by drying chestnuts, beating or grinding them into meal and baking like corn cakes. It was said to be a very good substitute for corn, very rich. (Which reminds me that Rev. Riley Doty of Arkansas once told me that his parents in Missouri made bread from sweet acorns during the Civil War. JTA)

A substitute for coffee was made by browning whole wheat and grinding it on the coffee mill, or by browning corn meal and boiling as coffee. (I have tasted "coffee" made from meal—I hope the wheat was better. JTA)

Men would go to saltpetre caves and gather the saltpetre to be used for a substitute for salt.[11]

∽ ∾

DRIED PUMPKIN

DRIED PUMPKIN WAS one of the most widely used foods back when I was a boy and ever since people settled in this country. Every farmer planted pumpkins among his corn and the fields would be dotted with the yellow pumpkins in the fall. There was also many of the cushaw sorts grown. With the coming of frost the pumpkins were gathered in, most times they would be gathered along with the corn and piled under a shed at the crib. Then a little later the entire family would put in several hours after supper each night peeling and cutting the pumpkins into strips which were placed on sticks and these were rested on joists or other supports and the pumpkins dried in the shade. The way the pumpkin drying was carried out was by cutting the pumpkin open in the middle and removing the seeds and "guts" and then the halves would be cut into rings about an inch thick, these were then peeled and strung on the sticks. When being prepared for eating the strips were broken into pieces about an inch long and cooked with fat bacon. The bacon was said to be the best way meat could be cooked.[12]

∽ ∾

MAKING FLESH OF LIVING ANIMALS

I DON'T KNOW WHERE you'd want this one or not, but I know of people living on meat from hogs that was still alive. I've heard 'em tell of a man in Tazewell county named Moore who had a habit of going over the country an' changing boar hogs for farmers. This feller carried a bucket with 'im an' when he cut a hog he'd save the seeds he took out an' take 'em home with 'im an' eat them. His wife an' children eat 'em too.*

I've heard of other people eatin' hog seeds. They say that there's a feller at Wise that changes hogs an' all he charges is the seeds.

*[Note from JTA] I personally knew John Moore in Tazewell County, referred to by Mr. Kilgore. He was a so-called "good-liver" of the Flat Top section. Once served as deputy U.S. Marshal for Tazewell County. Considered a leading citizen of the county. Owned a large hill farm. I rented a house of him for about six months in 1920, and lived within five hundred yards of his home. I know that he practiced "working on hogs" as he called it and took the seeds as his pay, or at least he took them and had them cooked and he and his family eat them. I recall that he had a fuss with a school teacher who was boarding with the family, because she refused to pertake of the dish.[13]

Nicholson Hollow in the Shenandoah National Park Area, Virginia. October 1935. John [T.] Nicholson peeling apples. Farm Security Administration Photographer Arthur Rothstein. [LC-USF34-00360-D].

AN UNUSUAL FOOD DISH

A VERY UNUSUAL food dish that is prepared in the Cumberland mountain section and one that is quite widely used here is that of fried Poke, from the pokeweed (Phytolacca decandra [probably Phytolacca americana]). This dish is sometimes called "dry land fish" due to it's slight fishy taste. Early in the spring after the new shoots or sprouts have come from the roots they are gathered while still young and tender, peeled, sliced and parboiled for about ten minutes. Then they are taken from the hot water, rolled in corn meal, salted and peppered to taste and then fried in deep fat until very brown.

These tender poke shoots are also gathered and prepared like asparagus and eaten. The young shoots when prepared look very much like asparagus tips. It is also gathered while tender and used as greens.

Many of the mountain wives gather these tender shoots in the spring and can them for winter use. For canning they are peeled, sliced and parboiled until tender. Then taken from the water placed in the jars and covered with scalding water, with either a small amount of salt or acid being added to each jar.[14]

∽ ∾

APPLE PEELING TIME IN THE COUNTRY

WE ALWAYS HAD a good time in the country at apple and peach peelin' time.

When a family got ready for this they'd always get up the fruit and wash it. Then they'd send word round to the neighbors that they was goin' to have a peelin' that night.

Everybody would have early supper and come on to the peelin'.

We'd most of the time set out in the yard cause most folks would have a table outdoors to eat on when 'twas warm enough and 'twas convenient to put the fruit on.

There'd be plenty of lanterns to work by if it 'twasnt' a bright night. 'We'd set and peel and talk and laugh and everybody would have a good time.

The young folks and the old folks would come too.

Nicholson Hollow in the Shenandoah National Park Area, Virginia.
October 1935. [John] Russ Nicholson peeling apples. Farm Security
Administration Photographer Arthur Rothstein. [LC-USF34-00363-D].

At our house we had a scaffold outdoors with planks laid over it and whenever there was a large panfull ready somebody would go and empty the fruit out on this after paper has been spread over the planks.

The fruit was kept out like this till it dried and then put in clean cloth bags.

My mother always saved the salt bags for this.

After the fruit was bagged 'twas brought in and put in the room upstairs and throwed across the 'wind beams' to keep it all right.

At these peelin' parties everybody enjoyed themselves—there was no cussin' or fussin' and fightin'. It was a old fashion good time and before the folks left somebody was more'n apt to say they was goin' to have a peelin' and everybody was invited.

Same way with the pea-shellin' after the peas got dry. We'd all get together agin.

Before the peas was put away we'd always get the trash and dry pieces of hulls out by spreadin' out a sheet on the ground and somebody would stand and pour the peas out and as they was fallin' somebody else would stand by and fan them out and the trash would be separated before the peas fell on the sheet.

I've seen peas poured out like this and if the wind was blowin' strong enough it would just blow all the trash away from the peas.[15]

∽ ∾

EVOLUTION OF BREAD MAKING IN WISE COUNTY

THE WAY HIT WAS here I guess hit was all over the country. Take right here at Big Glades, or Wise as hit's called now, an' old man Brown lived there an' he had a mortar to beat his corn into meal. I've seed mortars. They made 'em different ways, but usually they'd cut a trough in a big log an' make a sweep by putting a forked stake in the ground an' burn or bore holes through both forks right fernence one another an' also through a long pole about middleways. Then they'd put the long pole in the forks an' fasten hit thare by runnin' a rod of iron through the holes. The big or butt end of the pole was allus put on the *yan side* of the log that had the trough cut out in it. Then they'd put a rope or little pole to the little end of the big pole straight up over the trough an' fix a big block to it. The block was cut out jes to fit into the trough. Then they'd put, oh about a peck o' corn in the trough an' lift up on the little pole an' let loose an' let hit fall onto the corn an' hit'uz jes *beaty-to-beat* for hours an' hours tell the corn was beat into meal. Then they would take it out an' put in more corn. Slow way of gittin' bread but hit beat *grittin'*.

Oh yeah, grittin'. Everybody depended on grittin' for bread durin' the early fall. An' I've heard papa say that he'd knowed people to grit the year round. They'd sof'en the years of corn by b'ilin' 'em in pots an' kettles. Gosh, I used to hate to see meal time come. Cause they allus made us boys grit. Kept my fingers an' hands tore all to pieces. Way papa made a gritter was to take an' ol' bucket or can an' split hit open an' flatten hit out good, then he'd take a nail or awl an' punch holes in hit. The holes all were punched through one way an' the edges of the holes'ud be turned out an' sharp an' this was the grittin' surface. When one got dull or wore out they'd make another. There was two types or styles of gritters made. Some made 'em one way, some another. Most common was to take an ordinary board or piece of plank an' cut a long hole through it, oh, about a foot long en' inch and a half or two inches wide. Then nail the gritter right flat over this. The dough or meal, which ever you want to call hit, fell through this slit or hole. I've seed 'em grit soft ros'en years [roasting ears] an' I've seed 'em grit *pyorely* ol' hard corn. The other way they made a gritter an' a easer way was to jes sorty crimp up the piece of tin, rounding like, an' run a gritter stick between it an' the board an' let the meal run out at the lower end. You could't use this sort o' gritter a settin' down. Had to stan' up an' put ag'in yo' stomach an' 'tother end in the pan or tray. Hardly anybody ever eat anything but corn bread back then.

After awhile ol' man Brown, he rigged up a hoss mill out there, an' everybody took their grindin' there. His hoss mill looked jes like a canemill. Had a long sweep an' he'd hitch a hoss or mule to the end of it an' hit'ud go roun' an' roun' an' everytime hit'ud go roun' the rocks'ud go roun' several times, cause he had 'em geared up so they'd turn by cogs faster than the hoss went roun'.

"Twund't long then tell uncle John Addington put in a water mill here.
Hit was an' undershot wheel. He went an' cut a big poplar log an' cut
holes through it *slanchways* for the water to hit an' go through. Man
hit must a been a slow an' *teagious* job, but they had plenty of time back
then. The wheel set down under the mill an' when he'd raise the gate
an' turn the water on hit, hit'ud hit these holes an' ag'in the alopin' sides
an' turn the wheel. A shaft run from the center of the wheel up in the
mill house an' the bottom rock was fastened tight on hit. The top rock
didn't turn. The corn was dumped in the hopper above the rocks an'
dropped out one or two grains at a time down in the hole in the middle
of the top rock an' went between the two rocks. Hit'uz ketched in there
an' groun' into meal an' come out on one side into a box or sometimes
into the sack hooked on two pegs or nails. Some mills had the top rock
to turn en' the bottom one to lie still, but most of 'em had bottom rock
to turn. The feed could be increased or decreased by jes turnin' a
little knob or bolt that had a *whang* or string tied to it that raised it or
lowered it.

So that's the way people made out tell they got to buildin' big water-
mills an' steam mills started to come about. Jimmie Day brought the
fust steam mill in this country. An' hit'uz a show, too. People that didn't
have no business went for miles an' miles to see hit, an' they said that
when the engine popped off steam hit'ud nearly scare some of 'em to
death.[16]

∽ ∾

BISCUIT BEATERS

A BISCUIT BEATER is an iron rod, about 18 inches long, weighing 5
pounds. This was made at a blacksmith shop and was used in making
what was called "beaten biscuits". A block was sawed out of a sweet
gum tree and trimmed down until it was about four feet tall. The dough
was made up, put on the block and beaten with the iron rod. After the
dough had been beaten until it blistered it was taken and made into
biscuits. These were served hot for breakfast and supper, and on
Sunday night they were usually cold.[17]

FOX-KNOTS

THERE WAS ONE custom Grandma never failed to keep, and all of her daughters kept it up, and one of my sisters still does to this day—that was to fry 'fox-knots' every Shrove Tuesday, because if you didn't fry them on that day and use plenty of lard in the pan, then you would not get enough lard when you butchered to last you through the year . . . They were made something like doughnuts, only the dough was rolled real thin, cut in narrow strips, and dropped into deep, hot lard. They'd brown so crisp and delicious in a minute! My sister can make them just as good, and usually does fry them on Shrove Tuesday. I think she sorta half way believes in the superstition herself, but that may be because she still lives on a farm and is afraid to risk not getting her lard, in case there should be anything to that old saying. ["Fox-knots" is a corruption of *faschnacht*, a term for the fried cakes traditionally prepared on Shrove Tuesday and related to "pancake day" in England and similar traditions elsewhere—"faschnacht" or "fast-night" for the day preceding Ash Wednesday, which was a day of strict fasting in many areas.]

[The interviewer's mother was sitting in on the interview and got out an old cookbook copyrighted in 1901 by the Brethren Publishing House and produced the following recipe from Sister Amy Roop of Westminster, Maryland.]

> Fastnacht Cakes: *take 3 eggs, 2 cups of sugar, 1 cup of lard, 1½ pints sour milk, 1 teaspoonful of soda, 1 teaspoonful of cream of tartar, and enough flour to roll nicely. Cut and bake in boiling lard.*[18]

༄ ༄

HOME-MADE SAUSAGE CURED IN CORN SHUCKS

TALKIN' 'BOUT GOOD old home-made sausage, 'tain't none good like dat put up in corn shucks.

Course dis goes 'way back to de old days when folks had sumpin' to eat sho 'nough.

After de shucks done sorter dried and de ear of corn been took out, you dampens de shucks so dey will sorter give—den you packs de sausage already seasoned, down in de shucks and twists de shucks 'round de sausage 'till hit's all covered up—den you ties dis up close and swings hit up in de jice [joist].

Hit cures in dem shucks and dats de best sausage you kin ever git. All dis new style stuff, 'tain't nothin' to hit.[19]

∾ ∾

SALIT WEEDS

Dock: DOCK IS ONE of the two early cooking salits. It has large thick dark green leaves. The root is used to make a salve to cure fall sores (dew poison). It grows in fertile bottoms mostly.

Dandelion: This is the other of the early salits. It has small notched leaves and somewhat resembles mustard. The first flower to bloom in the spring. The root of this salit herb is used for many diseases and complaints, among these are gravel, kidney disorders and nervous diseases. It grows in rich coves and along streams.

Bear Lettice: The first of the killing down sorts (that is, served by pouring hot grease over it). This plant grows in hollers and swags usually among rocks. The leaf is oval shaped and the under side is purple. It is never cooked.

Crow's Foot: Another of the killing down sorts. Grows in rich coves in the woods. Has finely cut leaf in shape of a crow's foot, dark green in color.

Shonny: The most sought after of all killing down salits. It grows in rich coves and along streams under shade of trees or shrubs. The plant resembles the violet, but is larger and the shade is a lighter green.

Uncle Simpson's Lettice: Next to shonny it is most popular of the killing down sorts of greens or salits. It grows in rocky places where the soil is very fertile and in the shade. The plant is small, three-cornered leaves, and light colored.

Groundhog Salit: Groundhog salit grows in old fields and around barns and rock piles. It, too, resembles violets in form of growth, but has thicker leaves and is of tougher texture. It is one of the cooking sorts.

Nar Dock (Narrow Dock):   Nar Dock is not as early as the broadleaf variety, but is more sought after when it does appear. It is believed to have medical value in the cure of liver diseases. It is the leaves which are used, being cooked for greens or salit and eaten by the patient. Others eat it for its food value. The plant resembles the broadleaf dock, other than the leaves are very narrow and pointed and a darker green.

Plantin: Grows everywhere. There are two plantins, the salit plantin and the white which is used for medical purposes. The salit plantin is a low-growing plant, the leaves, a dark green lie flat on the ground. In early spring it is much sought for greens, but later in the season it becomes tough and is used only if other sorts are not to be found. It is cooked. This salit plantin is used to bind to boils and wounds in the same manner as pawpaw leaves are used, that is the leaves are wilted by holding close to the fire and then placed on affected part.

Stagger Weed: Not many people use stagger weed for salit, but some prefer it to any others. It derives its name from the manner in which cattle act after eating the root. Cattle are fond of the herb and in feeding on it they sometimes pull up the root and it is said that one small root will kill a cow. People who use it for salit are very careful not to get any of the root in the pot. The plant grows in deep coves and in very rich soil under shade of timber. Crowsfoot grows in the same locations and it is difficult for the average person to tell one from the other. The stagger weed usually grows more rank than crowsfoot.

Old King Cure-All: This plant grows mostly in low bottoms or on sandy hills. Like "plantin" it is a low growing plant, the leaves lying on the ground. It has striped leaves, green and light red, very narrow. The root is used for the treatment of almost all diseases known to man, which gives the name of "Old King Cure-All". It is also known as wild sweet potato, although it does not resemble a sweet potato in any way. The leaves are cooked for greens.

Polk: Polk is the most widely used salit plant in the Cumberlands, although the pioneer settlers thought it was poison and it was not until the industry of coal mining brought in outsiders that they began eating it. Polk is peculiar in that it does not grow in the wild state. That is it is seldom found where there has not been a clearing made in the forest. But a clearing may be made miles from the nearest polk plant and a brush heap burned and the plant will spring up in profusion. It grows to eight or ten feet tall, but only the young tender shoots are used for salit.

Milkweed: Milkweed is not so widely used for food, but some people gather a few plants to use with other salit weeds. (It might be well to state here that one [usually] "picks" a "mess' of only one sort of plant but [mixes plants when cooking]. Polk is usually cooked alone). Milkweed grows to a tall plant, but it is only the young tender plants which are used for greens. It gets its name from the milk-like substance which flows from the plant when broken. It usually grows in low and rich soil.

Lady's Finger: Lady's Finger grows in damp rich ground, usually along banks of small streams. It springs up with only two leaves, but has such rapid growth that in two days it is large enough to gather for salit. The leaf is long and dark green with a red splotch on top side which has the appearance that a woman has dipped her finger in blood and touched it.

Lamb's Quarter: This plant is one of the most popular of the wild salits. It grows in gardens or fields which have been plowed. The leaf is almost round and has the look as if to touch them they would fall to pieces.

Lamb's Tongue: Grows in low damp places and has a long narrow pink leaf, which accounts for the name.

Sissle: This is one of the most popular cooking salits. While the name may be a corruption of thistle it is no kin to that pest weed. It grows around old buildings and boulders. Seems to require a fertile soil. It is low growing and in habit of growth resembles dandelion, only the leaves are darker and more crisp and crinkly.

Red Worms: As far as I can learn this seems to be an exclusive Adams family diet. Mrs. Carter is the only person outside of my immediate family who knew it, and she was a Miss Adams before her marriage. The plant grows in deep and rich coves and flats, usually in high but damp places. It will be found growing in very early spring in beds, always in deep shade and on ground that has not been cleared or cultivated. The plant is very slight in growth and the stem is long and slender with two slim leaves about an inch long. The under side of the leaf and the stem are a deep pink color which gives it the name "Red Worms." It is gathered by pulling it up, and the roots, which are long, slender and also pink, are also saved for food. It is not a cooking salit, but is prepared by cutting up (sometimes with green onions) and wilted with hot grease.

Sheep Sorrel: Most women out salit-picking try to find a few bunches of sheep sorrel for flavoring the "mess." It grows on the very thinnest soil usually around old stumps or rocks. The plant resembles clover, only that it is much lighter. Sometimes it is used to make pies and such pies are similar to rhubarb pies. Children hunt the plant for its sweet, candy-like roots.

Old Field Mustard: A low growing plant found in abandoned or outlying fields. Like the cultivated mustard it has a pungent flavor and it is added to other green plants to impart flavor. In habit of growth it resembles the garden mustard only that the leaves are more finely cut.[20]

༄ ༅

DRY JAM

DRY JAM USED to be one of the most popular foods here in the mountains. My mother made it and we hardly ever was without jam the year round. But in these times people have plenty of fruit jars to put up stuff in and you never see dry jam any more. It is the one food that has completely played out. I don't know of any other but what you occasionally see some of it, but dry jam is never seen any more. And it was as good if not better than the sort they put in cans now. Here is how ma made it. She would pick blackberries and raspberries, but mostly blackberries as they were more plentiful. She would look at them carefully just as if she was going to can them. Then she would cook them slightly. Mash into a mass and make out into cakes about half as big as a saucer and place on boards, which was called jam boards and which had been dressed smooth for that purpose, and lay these boards in the sun to dry. It usually took about four or five days to dry. The boards were made from ordinary clapboards like was used to cover houses and were smoothed with a pocketknife or a drawing knife. When the cakes were dry they were put in pokes and tied up and hung up against the wall. When needed for use the cakes were put in a pan or other container and a little water added and recooked. And believe me it was good eating.

(My mother followed the same method in making dry jam. I have assisted her in making it, and I remember that it seemed months instead of days for it to cure in the sun, JTA).[21]

∽ ∾

OLD-TIME POUND CAKE

WELL, TO BEGIN with, my mother learnt how to make them cakes years ago when she was a young woman from one of them old-time nigger cooks. Her name was Tishie Lewis and she baked cakes for all them rich folks in Milton, North Carolina. She was known far and near as, "Tishie Lewis, the Cake Baker from Milton, North Carolina."

Helpin' my mother to make 'em learnt me how too.

She weighed one pound flour, one pound butter, and one pound sugar and used ten eggs.

She chipped or sorta cut up the butter in small pieces and worked in that pound of sugar with her hands until hit was light and creamy. It taken a long time to get hit like that.

Then she would put in the yellows of the eggs and keep on mixin' up with her hands. Them yellows she would beat up with a spoon before she put 'em in—and the whites with a fork. We never used a egg-beater. Then comes a little of the whites and a little of the flour 'till all of hit was used up. Many a time I've done seen that pound of flour measured out and settin' in front of the fire to warm it up before she mixed hit in.

If the butter was just about salty enough she wouldn't add anymore to the batter and if you liked a little lavering you could put in some.

She baked her cake in a pan where had the tube in the middle and always greased hit with lard and then sprinkled flour over it and struck or knocked the pan to shake off the loose flour.

She would set the pan in a iron oven with a lid on it in the open fireplace and fire it up a little at a time, puttin some live coals under the oven a little at a time. After hit done rose all hit's goin' to and about time for hit to brown she fired it from the lid—a little—to make hit brown.

Hit would take about two and one-half hours to bake that cake right.

After she took hit up and let hit cool she would wrap hit in a clean cloth and put in a clean lard can with the top on close. When I was young and fresh I could bake a good cake too, but seems like I done lost my nerve.

(Miss Stevens said, "A cake like that won't ever make you sick and it sets jest as good on the stomach." She showed [me] the cake pan used in her family for over 60 years).[22]

꿍 꿍

A BARREL OF PERSIMMON BEER
FOR CHRISTMAS

I THINKS ONE of the things we all enjoyed the most bout Christmas time was havin' a barrel of 'Simmon Beer' to drink made at home— and 'twas bout the only thing we had them days to pass round when company comed in. We'd draw it from the barrel in a pitcher or bucket and fill the glasses and look like everybody sho' did enjoy it.

Ma was a great hand to make it and she made hers with simmons and these locusts where folks eat. Course you know you haves to let the frost bite 'em both befo' you ken use 'em and she washed 'em good befo' she started to makin' the beer.

If you makes the beer early in the fall you can use the simmons like they is but they won't keep fresh till bout three week befo' Christmas— thats the time we all made the Christmas beer—so to have the simmons to use Ma used to make up what she called a 'Simmon Pone' like this:

Mix up some bran and water and then you puts in as many simmons as you ken and stirs it jest like a thick puddin'. Then put this in deep pans and things and put in the stove and bake jist like a puddin'. I've seen 'em bake 'em so hard that when they was ready to use some of them pones to make the beer they'd have to break 'em up with a axe.

They'd use a good size wooden barrel with a bung-hole and they'd start by puttin' some clean straw—bout a big handful round the bung-hole on the inside of the barrel for to strain the beer as it comed out.

Then they'd put in a layer of simmon pone, then a layer of locusts—break the locusts in pieces—and they kept on doin' this till the barrel was full plumb up to the top. Then put the water in till it shows up at the top of the barrel. Jest put the top on and let it stand and after it be done worked, you sho got a good drink. You can't get drunk on simmon beer and its a healthy drink too.

I've seen 'em at home haves the loft full of locusts ready to use. Whenever Ma heared tell of a locus tree anywheres round, she'd hitch up the wagon and go after them locusts, maybe two or three miles off.

We got the simmons and locusts out'n the woods.[23]

∽◦ ◦∾

ENGLISH WASSAIL BOWL

ANCIENT NAME WAS One Yard of Flannel. Heat one quart of ale almost to the boiling point. Into it stir some grated nutmeg, powdered ginger, and the peel of one lemon. While the ale is heating beat up three eggs with four ounces of moistened white sugar. Then put the hot ale into the beaten sugar and eggs in one pitcher, and into another pitcher put a quart of good old rum or brandy. Turn these ingredients back and forth from one pitcher into another until the mixture is smooth, then pour into the holly-wreathed Wassail Bowl. Heat all containers thoroughly beforehand. Serve hot.

Make of the richest wines, with roasted apples bobbing about on top.

All drink from this bowl, wishing to all present a Merry Christmas, pronouncing it the ancient fountain of good feeling where all hearts met together.

At "Bridgewater Plantation" always at Christmas time the English gardener (who lived and worked many years on this plantation) by the name of Charles Hindley from Chester, England, made the English Wassail Bowl by this recipe. His Wassail Bowl's became famous, and he served the gentry of the countryside. This recipe was copied from an old portfolio dated 1861.[24]

❦ ❦

BIRCH BEER

WHEN I WAS A BOY everybody made birch beer to drink at the table instead of milk. Most people liked it better than butter milk. It was good all right. The way they made it was by tapping a birch tree or trees and in the same way that sugar trees were tapped. They caught the sap in troughs or buckets, mixed corn meal with it and let it set till it worked and then strained it. People would sometimes drink birch beer and become drunk on it. It seemed to have quite a kick.[25]

❦ ❦

TEAS FOR THE TABLE

[Note by JTA]: The pioneers in the Cumberlands used many barks, herbs and roots for making tea to drink at meals, substitutes for coffee and sometimes for milk. The most popular tea was made from the bark of sassafras root. This, as well as some others, are still used by people in the more isolated parts, not so much as a necessity but simply because the people like it, preferring it to coffee or imported teas sold in the stores.

I remember that I hired to Elihu Stallard to hoe corn one summer. His wife worked in the field along with the other hands, but, as was the custom, she would go to the house about ten thirty to cook dinner for the others. Every morning Stallard would grub a good sized sassafras root and lay it at the end of field and Mrs. Stallard would take it to the house and make tea for dinner. He would always caution her, "Don't forget the tea root," when she started to leave the field.

Sassafras: Law yes, we used to drink *sassafack* (common name here) tea twice a day an' sometimes for breakfast. I like hit. We drunk hit mostly when we was workin' our corn out. They'd be sassafack a-growin' at the edge of the field an' pa would grub up one or two an' we'd take 'em to the house an' wash 'em an' peel the bark off an' put hit in a tea kettle or jes a plain kettle an' bile hit tell hit was strong as we liked hit. Some folks liked hit purty strong an' others not so strong, jes like they do coffee. We'd sweeten hit with molasses. Hardly ever had any sugar, but I liked hit better when hit was sweetened with molasses. Boy, I tell ye hit'uz good. I make hit yet sometimes. Hit'uz healthy, too. My 'pinion is 'f more people'ud drink sich as that now 'stead o' so much coffee an' stuff they'd be a sight healthier. Hit's good for the blood an' stomach.

Spicewood: Next to sassafack tea I guess spicewood tea was used more 'an any other. Ye made hit jes like ye did sassafack only ye used the little twigs an' limbs. Broke 'em up in little short pieces so ye could get 'em in the kettle an' bile 'em tell ye got all the strength out or as much as ye wanted. A lot o' people liked hit better 'an sassafack, but me, I allus liked sassafack the best. They sweetened spicewood with molasses, too. Ye know spicewood is a mighty good remedy for the measles. Break 'em out nearly every time. (Spicewood is a small, grey-bark shrub growing about five feet.)

Mountaintea: One o' the best tasted teas they is is mountaintea tea. Gee hits the best stuff ye ever tasted in yo' life. Hit'uz not drunk as much as sassafack an' spicewood, but hit shore is good. Ye jes gather some o' the mountaintea leaves. Ye know hit grows 'round on pore ivy p'ints. Bile hit an' sweeten it. Don't take much sweetenin' either. Hit's sweet anyhow. Us kids used to make hit an' keep hit jes to drink when we wanted hit, not at the table.

Maple Tea: Not many people made tea out o' sugar trees an' maples, but hit'uz good. Too good to waste in tea I guess. I've drunk hit. Tastes nearly like mountaintea tea. I've knowed people to make hit when they'uz makin' sugar or molasses in the winter time. Guess one reason why people did't use hit more'n they did was because they couldn't make only in winter time.

Liverwort: Liverwort (trailing Arbusus) makes a mighty good tea too, but one thing hit's scace an' another hit's saved mostly for makin' tea for liver trouble an' other ailments. Hit grows on pore ivy p'ints mostly an' runs on the groun' sorty like groun' ivy. Hit has the purtiest little blossom on hit ye ever seed in yo' life; a little bluish pink blossom, sorty bell-shaped. They used the leaves for tea an' sweetened hit, but hit didn't need so much molasses an' hit tastes awful good.

Birch: Some ol' people made tea out o' birch bark or the juice. They'd tap the trees an' boil it jes like they did sugar trees. I never drunk any birch tea, but my folks used to make birch beer an' we'd drink hit instead o' buttermilk. They'd tap the trees an' catch the juice an' put corn meal in it an' let hit work an' then drink hit.

Ginger: Nearly ever'body used to drink ginger tea, but o' course they made hit out o' brought-on-ginger roots they'd buy at the store. Hit'uz good. Next to sassafack I liked hit the best.[26]

∽ ∾

BEE HUNTIN'

LIKE THE FELLER said, I'uz jes countin' up the other day. I've found a hundred an' one or a hundred an' two bee trees in my life. Very well remember the first one I found. Pa kept bees an' fooled with 'em. Never was afraid of 'em. If they stung me they didn't hurt me. Been stung all over. Never swelled much from bee stings.*

One day when I was about twelve years old I went up on the Sally Dock Ridge an' put me out some bait. I used the same bait then I do now. I've never found anything to beat sweet anis an' sugar syrup. I spread it on under side of maple leaves an' lay the leaves on a bush. That's what I did that day. Wudn't more'n fifteen minutes tell here come a bee, then more. I lined 'em right out the ridge torge the Dean place. Put out my bait ag'in. Here they come, stronger 'n ever. As the feller said, 'I lined 'em three times 'fore they turned back. Oh, yeah, I mean by turnin' back that when ye keep movin' yo' bait in one direction till the bees start coming the other way. Then I knowed I'd passed 'em. So I sarched aroun', lookin' in the trees 'tween the last two places I'd put down the bait an' wudn't long tell I seed 'em goin' in an' out of a limb way up on a big chestnut. Boy! I'uz the best tickled boy right then that ever lived.

'Member one time Luther Rogers, poor ol' Luther's dead now. Fell dead out here at Glamorgan. He sent Bill over one day an' said he wanted me to come over on the Poor House Branch an' find a bee tree fer 'im. They'd found 'em waterin' at George Gardner's, but had hunted a solid week an' couldn't find 'em. So I went the next day. Got there about one o'clock. Put out my bait, seed they was goin' across a p'int. In less than an hour I'd found 'em in a big forked chestnut they'd looked in a dozen times. Took me a long time to git them to see 'em after I found 'em. Luther said, "A man that can see as good as you, I'm jes goin' to give ye the tree. Frank Kilgore an' Jim Gardner helped cut it. Got two zinc bucket fulls of honey out of it. Richest tree I ever seed.

One time Johnny Stapleton an' Bobby Roberts had a course up above Big John Edinton's. They had been huntin' for over a week. I'uz passin' one day an' they said they'uz two trees they knowed 'cause part of 'em was yellow ones an' part black ones. The yeller ones went one way an' was gone about four minutes. (Bees are timed by the hunters by sprinkling flour on their wings while at the bait). The black ones went the other way an' was gone about ten minutes. So I hit out after the black ones first. Moved the bait up an' in a half an hour I had 'em turned aroun'. Wudn't more'n ten minutes till I found 'em. Then I pitched in on the yellow ones an' found them in less than fifteen minutes. I never even put out bait for them. I jes sunned 'em. Way I sun 'em is to git 'em between me an' the sun. Dennis Riner said one time that I could see a honey bee furder 'an he could see a turkey buzzard. Forgot to say I had to foller them black bees over two miles. They went back across Buck Knob by the wild hog pen (Built by the late James Monroe "Jeems" Roberts in which to corral his hogs that had been on the mast).

Floyd Cox was said to be the best bee hunter ever in this country. 'Member one time he found a tree for Raleigh Kilgore. Raleigh had been huntin' for hit all summer. Had 'em coursed, but couldn't find 'em. He'd even found em waterin', an' ye know bees water at the nearest water. So when ye find 'em waterin' ye'll know they hain't fer off. But Raleigh couldn't find that tree an' he said to be pritty good at findin'

bees hisse'f. So when Floyd come an' found hit, he couldn't show hit
to Raleigh. Raleigh jes couldn't see hit. Was in a big tall chestnut. Raleigh
had looked at hit a hundred times I guess. He wouldn't b'leve they'uz
in thar till they cut hit down, an' thar they was goin' right in at the top
of the tree, where hit had been a little limb broke off.

*[Note by JTA] This may sound like a tall tale, but I found a bee tree in Arkansas
once (only one I ever found) and after I had hived them, I picked 111 bee
stings elsewhere on my body and I did not swell at all. But three days later
one yellow jacket stung me on end of my finger and my hand swelled fit to
burst and my face swelled till my eyes were almost closed.[27]

∽ ∾

TALE ABOUT A MOLASSES BOILING

SPRING RAINS WERE POURING in the mountains. The men [unable to
work] had here-gathered on top a yard square plateau where stood the
log-bodied store and post office building. The men sat around, spit-
ting amber (tobacco juice) on the hot stove and telling tales.

"Remember that cane bilin at Buck's last fall," ventured Tom, veteran
joker. A shout of laughter went up while Buck's face grew as red as the
side of the stove.

"Cut a-loose with th' yarn," yelled Sam.

"My brother Odie an' Buck here jined in er partner bargain ter raise
sorg'um on th' 'flue patch' at Odie's. Hit was er handy place ter grow
th' cane, nigh th' flue what war already built fer biling th' juice. An' th'
'morter hole' wha they'd dug out th' clay ter build th' chim'ly with, wus
tha too. Hit's [now been] turned ter 'skimming hole,' wha they put th'
scum from th' biling sorg'um juice.

"Folks come from far an' nigh ter th' biling. Buck thought he'd raise
some fun. He kivered th' 'skimming hole' with boards an' bresh so's
nobody wouldn't see hit come night.

"Th' young folks come nigh dusk-dark, an' had er play-party outdoors. Buck had went home an' put on his 'tow' (flax) home spun pants.
Them pants war his best outfit o' clothings. They done played 'Shoot
the Buffalo' an' 'Skip-Ter-My-Lou" till they wus clean wore out. An' what
with ah-tasting o' th' sweet juice they'd got powerful thirsty.

"Buck an' th' girl he was talkin' ter (courting) led th' way ter th' spring. Th' path went nigh past th' 'skimming hole' what Buck had done clean forgot all ah-bout. His white pants was a shining in th' firelight. All of er sudden, Buck let out er screech same as er kittymount (catamount) had him. He choked like er cow what had swollered er turnup, an' thrashed ah-round in the 'skimming hole' like a dozen rattlers.

"What th' hell is I in?" Buck final'y [yelled] out.

"Buck come ah-scrambling out o' th' 'skimming hole' all ah dripping an' greenish. He tore off smack through th' bushes an' nobody never seed him fer er whole week."[28]

ഔ ഩ

SUGAR CANE BOILING— "SORGHUM MOLASSES"

THE CANE IS LEFT to fully mature, and not cut until just before time for frost. In this community, a mill for grinding the cane, will go the "rounds" among the neighboring families, just like the large copper kettles used for boiling apple butter, go from one house to another they being used only once a year, by each family, a cooperative spirit prevails; so when fall of the year comes, an agreement is reached so there will be no conflict in the time of boilings.

Usually two horses are kept alternating as necessary in the grinding, as the constant walking round and round makes the horse drunk, horses are changed quite often. Sometimes serious accidents occur, for in "feeding" the cane into the mill, if not careful one's hand will be caught, and if it so happens that no one is near to stop the horse, the hand may be badly crushed. Buckets are placed under the mill to catch the "juice" as the cane is ground, after the cane has all been ground, the boiling begins, a large iron kettle is used. Four "stout" poles are planted in the ground forming a square, then quilts are hung on three sides of these poles and fastened securely to keep out the chilly air, the sunny side is left open; the wood fire is then started under the big kettle, as much of the sweet syrup as the kettle will hold is poured in and the boiling begins.

The older folks finish one kettle at a time, as the syrup boils down, the latter day makers keep pouring in fresh juice which gives the sorghum that bitter taste, and dark greenish color. It requires many hours to boil, and has to be skimmed and skimmed continually up until it is finished and as it begins to thicken it has to be stirred also. Mrs. Mary Poage 78 years of age who lived on Back Creek Roanoke County, Virginia told the writer that her Grandmother told her to always put in a small amount of soda just before taking the molasses up, and this causes another, and final accumulation on top which has to be skimmed off, and also give the molasses a clear bright color.

Mrs. Luther Trout in talking with the writer, said she remembers at her mother's home as a child, standing around, and watching the girls with their big "bustles" on, stirring and skimming the molasses. The young folks always managed to get together and do a little courting on these occasions, as Mr. Trout remarked, "they did more courting than work," anyway, they brought fresh life and sparkle to the tired workers of the day. If there was a quantity of the syrup to be boiled it would last sometimes until quite late, and there would be dancing, and always refreshments.

This molasses was not made for market, but with much persistency sometimes a farmers wife in the old days, could be persuaded "to part" with a gallon or two. It was the families main source for supply of sweets, through the long winter days, and buck-wheat cakes which were usually made of Floyd County buck-wheat, were almost as large as a dinner plate, and these with sausage, and sorghum molasses made the country folks a sumptuous breakfast, with this meal always a cup of coffee, followed by a glass or two of milk. Without fail practically in every country home, on the breakfast, dinner, and supper table, will also be found the dish of apple butter, almost the year around.[29]

ᔕᔕ ᕼ

TREE MOLASSES AND SUGAR

USED TO BE THAT nearly everybody had some sugar trees (hard maples) on their places. Most of them are gone now. And they would make enough tree sugar for home use and some with lots of trees would make it to sell.

We had quite a sugar orchard. That's what large forests of maples were called. The way it was done was to either chop notches in the trees or bore holes in them with augers. The holes were best as they did not damage the tree so much as the chopped notches. If a hole was made then an elder was hollowed out and placed in the hole. Some cut a notch and then bored a hole just below the notch and let it connect with the notch; while some struck with axe just below notch and then led the sap from the notch down a narrow notch to a piece of board which had been drove into the opening.

The water was gathered about three times a day from the troughs and boiled in large pots until it was molasses or sugar as desired. The sugar was molded into teacup cakes, some in saucer cakes and some in egg-shells for the kiddies. It was sold to the country stores.[30]

∽ ∾

BUCKWHEAT CAKES AND TREE MOLASSES

IN THE EARLY part of the year 1885, just when the sap was rising in the maple (sugar maple) trees I was one of a company of young folks from the neighborhood of Orkney Springs, in Shenandoah county, who made a trip to Hardy County (just across the line) in West Virginia, near the Post Office of Matthias, where we were guests of a hospitable fami-ly which owned a lot of sugar maples, and grew on the place annually a crop of buckwheat. The flour from the buckwheat in this communi-ty, of course, was the genuine article—not bolted to tasteless powder but with all the natural elements and qualities of the grain retained ex-cept the hulks [husks] of the wheat. We saw and also ate the best "taf-fy" ever made, from the boiled-down sugar-tree sap, which was made by dipping the thickened syrup—before it was "done" enough for maple sugar—into a cup of water. At meal time we had "regular" West Virginia buckwheat cakes—dark in color—almost black, but oh, the tastiness, the relish one had for the delicious cakes— large enough to almost cover one's plate—well treated with good country butter and fresh maple syrup ("tree molasses"), and such as few today have the opportunity to en-joy. Nothing can excel this type of buckwheat cakes and made-in-the-community syrup—all pure as nature's alembic can make them, en-tirely unadulterated or unmixed with other and less tasty substitutes, of whatever source or kind. When eating such a fine product of country housewife skill, with materials furnished by the men of the family, one has the thrill of eating "what satisfies" as nothing else can.[31]

∽ ∾

AN APPLE BUTTER BOILING

THE INDUSTRY AND THRIFT of the early German settlers in the Shenandoah Valley were generally rigorous and invigorating habits. Many of these slightly modified habits or "customs" have been handed down through the years to the present. In rural districts of Frederick County, where "plantations" are dotted in checkerboard plots of farm land and orchard, farmers and their more sophisticated neighbors look to the dropping of the leaves with keen interest. Autumn, for the Valley farmer, means the harvesting of thousands of bushels of richly red apples. Packing sheds, where the ripened fruit is sorted by migrant workers for Fancy and US No. 1 markets, and the culls boxed for shipment to apple by-product plants, are beehives of sound and motion. Long convoys of trucks, groaning under the weight of their stacked bushel measures, move slowly along the roads and highways, converging upon Winchester, the mecca of orchardists in the northern section of Virginia.

Frost finds but little of the precious fruit wasted. Housewives throughout the section lug from their dusty hiding places great copper kettles. Cleared spaces in back yards are readied. With sand and pumice the copper kettles are scoured to a burnished gold color. Great stacks of fire wood—gathered by the younger boys and girls during the after school hours—appear mysteriously within reach of the gleaming kettles. And then the fun begins.

Kindly disposed neighbors are "invited in" after the farmer's day has drawn to an end. Bonnetted housewives and daughters—for the hours of peeling mean much festivity—descend upon the household, armed with paring knives and pails.

For days there has been much pie and cake making. Cider with a bite that brings a healthy rose color to the cheeks of young and old alike is stored in the pantries. Long tables are set in the living room—for many of the poorer homes boast only of a combined kitchen and living room—

and they are piled high with pumpkin pies, a rich creamy yellow in their fork-crimped crusts, mince pies, fragrant with spices and brandy, apple turnovers for the boys and girls, sugar sticks, gingerbread cookies made with "black strap" sorghum and filled with currants and raisins. Not infrequently the "lowly jug" occupies the center of the food ladened tables, for surely the men folk will find cider a tame companion. Hymns and the more bawdy mountain songs are sung. Jokes are told. Younger members of the family are stretched prone upon the floor, listening to the merriment of their elders, for upon this night they are permitted to remain up long past their usual bed time.

When sufficient apples have been pared and cored, and the revelers are weary of the fun, one by one, as the occasion may be, they take their leave. A neighbor lady, pausing at the front door for one last word, reminds her hosts that she will be on the job bright and early in the morning, for then begins the boiling and stirring.

Over the countryside, even before the roosters flaunt their raucous voices upon the frosty air, smoke from innumerable pot fires hangs in pungent clouds. Pots are filled with sweet cider and brought to a boil, then the apples are dropped in until the kettles are full. After hours of continuous stirring, during which more apples have been added to keep the pot full to a certain level, sugar, cinnamon and other spices are stirred into the rich, bubbling butter.

Night fall usually finds the butter being removed from the fires, now a rusty brown liquid permeating the air with its spicy aroma. It is dipped into stone crocks and jars and set aside to cool before being stored in pantries and cupboards.

Cold weather usually finds the Valley farmer with many gallons of apple butter stored away for use during the long winter months.[32]

∽ ∾

FOOD SERVED AT A CORN SHUCKING

A FARMER'S WIFE, in telling the writer of the preparation for the dinner, said cakes and pies were made in advance by the thrifty housewife. Without exception, in every interview with a farmer or his wife, mention has been made of chicken pie, or "chicken and dumplings;" this seems to have been the "piece-de-resistance." The writer met an old farmer at the market recently and in the conversation he said, "T'wouldn't have been a corn shucking without chicken and dumplings."

Another favorite dish was "possum and sweet potatoes" which they somehow always managed to have. Sour-Kraut was another dish that was enjoyed by many; always by the German families and especially when the dumplings were added. These dumplings were made of corn meal with a little soda added, salt, pepper, sugar, and a little baking powders, mixed with water and made into cakes and dropped in the Kraut just before it is ready to be served. A large dish of pork, and usually boiled cabbage, which was cooked with a generous piece of (salt) side meat. Potato salad seasoned with onions, cold slaw made of finely chopped cabbage, a "hard head" always being selected for slaw, a hot dressing was made and poured over this. There was plenty of cucumber pickle to give zest to the meal.

Now for the sweets: In answer to the question about the desserts, a farmer's wife, gave the writer a look of surprise and with an amused smile on her face asked: "Was there ever a man who didn't like apple pie?" And apple pie there was, although sweet potato custards were a close rival, and pumpkin pies were in the blue ribbon class also. In one of the farm houses, the writer was shown one of those "old time" high glass cake stands; on these occasions they were brought forth and stacked high with sliced cake. The universally liked apple butter was a never failing dish served in great deep round bowls.

The drinks consisted of—well—just before dinner a rather generous portion of apple brandy. Cider too, which had been boiled and allowed to get ice cold [was served]. Large cups of hot coffee were served with the dinner.

When the dinner hour arrived the men would come to the house and "wash up" out on the back porch and then would take a good drink before eating. The men always ate first. The ladies and girls waited on the table. You may be sure that the girls saw to it that their sweethearts had first choice of all the dishes passed around—this information volunteered by a great-grandmother.

J.J. Beheler of Roanoke told the following story:
The wife of a backwoods farmer had the reputation of being rather close. The morning following the corn shucking her husband walked out around the barn looking things over; his wife soon followed him. He turned and said to her: "Well, I'll tell you Katie, we've got some mighty good neighbors. Just look how well they've cleaned everything up, God bless 'em." His wife, with a heavy sigh, said: "Yes, everything in the kitchen is well cleaned up too, Gawd dam' 'em."[33]

∽ ∾

SERGEANT SAUNDERS' BRUNSWICK STEW

SOME TWENTY YEARS ago, the genial Mr. John G. Saunders, City Sergeant of Richmond, Virginia, inaugurated for the benefit of the American Legion, his "Sergeant Saunders' Brunswick Stews," which have since become legend in Virginia. Selling at fifty cents a quart, enough stew was sold upon this occasion to net the Legion five hundred dollars.

Since then Sergeant Saunders has made his famous stews for all the churches of all denominations and all the worthy charities that have sought to benefit from his great generosity.

When called upon for some worthy cause, Sergeant Saunders furnishes all the ingredients of the stew so that the price paid by the hundreds and sometimes thousands of people who attend these community events is practically clear profit.

Some idea of what a truly colossal feat of outdoor cooking is involved in the making of one of these stews may be realized from the following description. In 1930, a Richmond policeman was killed in line of duty. A committee of 35 citizens was formed to seek ways and means to materially demonstrate to his widow the appreciation of a grateful city. Sergeant Saunders responded to the call. A large vacant lot was selected for the site, and on the day of the event the great iron cauldrons were placed and the fires started.

Six hundred gallons were to be made and so into the pots Sergeant Saunders and his assistants put 240 veal shins, 12 beef shins, 780 pounds of chicken (live weight), 48 pounds of bacon, 1,800 pounds

Brunswick Stew, Brunswick County, Virginia. A view showing Mrs. J.E. Lewis filling quart jars with stew while Mr. J.E. (Tom) Lewis continues to stir the stew. Virginia State Library and Archives.[45.4443].

of Irish potatoes, 18 bushels of celery, 600 pounds of onions, 24 dozen bushels of carrots, 360 pounds of cabbage, 150 gallons of canned tomatoes, 72 gallons of canned corn, 48 pounds of butter, and the whole well seasoned with salt, pepper, and thyme.

For six hours the stew steams and bubbles and is constantly stirred, sending abroad its appetizing aroma that is its own advertisement for gathering the crowds that come at the appointed time to buy by the quart or gallon. It was upon this occasion that the last quart was auctioned off and bid in for ten dollars by Dr. Bright, who at that time was Mayor of Richmond. More than one thousand dollars was realized for the policeman's widow.

A conservative estimate indicates that at least $16,000 has been raised for good causes during the twenty odd years these sales of "Sergeant Saunders' Brunswick Stews" have been memorable events in Richmond.

Natives of Brunswick County no doubt would take exception to Sergeant Saunders' recipe, decrying the cabbage, and breathing anathema upon the substitution of bacon for squirrel, but then the little furry public pets in old Capitol Square are carefully guarded. And would it seem fitting for Richmond's beloved Sergeant to attempt to outwit the Capitol Police?[34]

The argument over "real" Brunswick stew is a hot one and continues to the present time. One story of its invention is as follows:

> One brisk day sometime around 1828, so the legends go, Dr. Creed Haskins, of Mount Donum on the Nottoway River [Brunswick County, Virginia], took several of his acquaintances hunting with him. Of course they took along "Uncle Jimmy" Matthews, who always cooked for Dr. Haskins' hunting expeditions. While everyone hunted, Uncle Jimmy spent his time shooting the fat, numerous squirrels that jumped through the oaks, and making a stew from them. The legend has it that the hunters, when they returned, were at first dubious of the stew in the pot, expecting rather a large roast. But on tasting Uncle Jimmy's concoction they exclaimed with wonder and asked for more when they were done.
>
> His original stew was made exclusively of squirrels, butter,

onions, stale bread, and seasoning. It fell to Dr. Haskins, according to Thomas Creed Haskins and Robert Creed Haskins, to add a little old brandy or Madiera to "give the stew a flavor."

In 1907 Meade Haskins wrote out the recipe his father, Dr. A.B. Haskins, had perfected:

> *Parboil squirrels until they are stiff (half done), cut small slices of bacon (middling), one for each squirrel; one small onion to each squirrel (if large, one to two squirrels), chopped up. Put in bacon and onions first to boil, while the squirrels are being cut up for the pot. Boil the above till half done, then put in butter to taste; then stale loaf bread, crumbled up. Cook then till it bubbles, then add pepper and salt to taste. Cook this until it bubbles and bubbles burst off. Time for stew to cook is four hours with steady heat.*

John P. Mason reported in 1907 that his family had a recipe handed down from Dr. Creed Haskins through Jack Stith to his father:

> *Start with six squirrels parboiled, add a quart of onions sliced, fat or bacon, and salt, red and black pepper. To thicken it, a pound of butter and breadcrumbs are added.* [35]

It must be true that Brunswick stew originated in Brunswick County, Virginia because, on February 22, 1988, Delegate R. Beasley Jones (D-Brunswick), mounted a podium in Brunswick County and read House Joint Resolution 35, which proclaims that the first Brunswick stew was cooked on the banks of the Nottoway River 160 years ago. This was done in order to put rival claimants from Brunswick County, Georgia and elsewhere in their proper place. [36]

∽ ∾

CHICKEN

THERE ARE MANY kinds of delicious food all over Virginia; but there is no food more valuable than the chicken; especially in the Northern Neck of Virginia. In this section one can find all kinds of good things

Brunswick Stew, Brunswick County, Virginia. Views showing the stew being sold at a rural auction in Brunswick County. The proceeds from the sale of this stew will go to the church. Virginia State Library and Archives. [45.11105].

to eat; crisp fried oysters, soft shell crabs, fish pudding, corn on the cob and all kinds of foliage food. But there is none which takes the place of the chicken on the family menu. There is an annual revival meeting at every church in the state and in the rural districts chicken assumes its proper place at these services. Here the sisters bring large baskets of food to church with chicken as the main course; chicken baked, fried, stewed, stuffed, and broiled. The very nature of the services demands chicken. After a half day of hilarious worship the services suddenly come to a halt. The chicken fat preacher will say; "Brother and sisters we all done had a great time in Zion dis mornin'; now we come to another important part of de services, a greater time-amen; I see de sisters got a heap lot of baskets out on de yard, I jest knows 'tis chicken in dem-amen: We all goin' out and eat-amen: After we done ate we will be in some shape to receive de holy ghost-amen: and specially if 'tis chicken we done et."

Soon the little church is empty and hundreds of people are standing around a long row of tables, made of old boards covered with snow-white sheets. In the center there is a large platter of chicken, sometimes a small wash tub full of chicken. The parson will ring his hands with a half hungry and holy-ghost look in his eyes and say: "Let us ask de blessin'. 'Lord, we knows 'tis a sin to kill but we kilt dese chickens for a purpose. Therefore we thank you for dis food, Lawd, 'cause dese chickens gave their lives that we might have meat, as you gave your life dat we might have salvation, we thank you Lawd-amen."

Then everybody reaches for the chicken. A dozen of the sisters at one time help the preacher's plate with a chicken leg. Sister Mary, the head Deacon's wife, is begging the pastor to have some of her chicken that was especially fried for him. Everybody is eating and happy when suddenly some sinner boy who has enough embarrasses everybody by yelling, "chicken ain't nothing but a bird."

There are Christians standing at the table, sitting on the grass, in automobiles; but all have chicken. There are certain unwelcome worshippers; flies, ants, dogs, cats, and even church mice attracted from miles around by the aroma of chicken. Legend says that the chicken is a holy bird, a gospel fowl. Country folk use the roosters instead of an alarm clock. If a rooster crows on the fence, it will clear and the rain is over; if he is on the ground there is sure to be a heavy rain; and if a rooster crows under a window, someone in the family is sure to die. These chicken worshippers say that in the spring time if a rooster sees a preacher coming he will warn all the chickens to hide and will declare war on the parson. I conclude that chicken is an indispensable food in Virginia.

Not for all, the crisp fried chicken, it might even be baked and some Cavalier might broil this holy bird, but not me, No, sir, as a preacher, I would not think of approaching the chicken house after dark—unarmed.[37]

✑ ✎

RECIPE FOR MAKING A GOOD SERVANT

Let the mistress of the house take two pounds of the very best self-control, a pound and a half of patience, a pound and a half of justice, a pound of consideration, and a pound of discipline. Let this be sweetened with charity, let it simmer well, and let it be taken in daily or (in extreme cases) in hourly doses, and be kept always on hand. Then the domestic wheels will run quite smoothly.[38]

✑ ✎

THE VIRGINIA OYSTER WAR

EVERYONE HAS HEARD that "music hath charms to soothe the savage breast [beast?]." But did you know that the lowly oyster has charms to turn an invading army into a host of friends? Well, it was proved in Gloucester County, Virginia, back in 1928. The incident is known as the Oyster War, but it was wholly bloodless.

The section of Gloucester County known as Guinea is inhabited by a people whose livelihood is obtained from the tidal waters that surround and penetrate the low-lying lands where they build their simple homes. They are a clannish folk, though hospitable, much inter-married,

wedded to their way of life and their immediate neighborhood, pas-
sionately antagonistic to any invasion of their rights. Fishing, clamm-
ing and oystering are their main pursuits. The Oyster War developed
in the winter of 1928 when the men of Guinea resisted what they considered an invasion of their vested right to tong for oysters in a section
of Mobjack Bay which the State Commission of Fisheries had leased
to a large planter.

This "rock," as such oystering areas are known, had been public
oystering ground from time immemorial, and the fathers and grand-
fathers of the present generation had tonged oysters there, as the men
of Guinea were doing, and proposed to continue doing regardless of
the big planter's lease. The power and dignity of the State could not
thus be flouted, and when the Guineamen's revolt progressed to the
point where the state patrol boat *Katy* was fired upon by Guineamen
concealed in the marshes, the Governor ordered several companies of
the Virginia National Guard to the scene, to preserve order and the rights
of the big lessee.

The soldiers arrived and pitched their tents in a dry field of
broomsedge near Severn Wharf, eight miles from the disputed oyster
beds. The natives watched them curiously but politely. The troops were
not enthusiastic about their mission. A few hotheads among the
Guineamen were for setting fire to the broomsedge field, but wiser
counsels prevailed. Instead of fighting the soldiers, they feasted them.

And what a feast: chiefly oysters. Oysters raw, and oyster stew; oysters
fried, and oysters roasted. Have you ever eaten oysters roasted in hot
coals and served to you in their still hot shells, from which you picked
them with a knife blade, or, better still, tipped the shell up in your hungry
mouth and just let the luscious meat slide in? If you have, you will know
the warring oystermen's strategy was perfect. The soldiers were no longer
disinterested, neutral, and somewhat nervous guardians of law and
order. They were the Guineamen's friends and partisans.

It is pleasant to know that no bloodshed followed the party, that the
troops were ordered home, a compromise was effected, and investiga-
tion was ordered, and the Guineamen were eventually restored to their
right to tong the "rock" their daddies and granddaddies had tonged
before them.[39]

AN OYSTER ROAST
DOWN ON THE LYNNHAVEN RIVER

SEVERAL YEARS AGO I was an invited guest at an Oyster Roast down on the Lynnhaven River, which was one of the most delightful events I ever attended.

The place was an estate called "Witch Duck" Farm. A large brick house sat back in a pretty grove on a knoll of a point overlooking one of the prettiest views of the Lynnhaven River. The lawn, green, well-kept, and sloping down to the river, presented quite a lovely scene in the early fall. In the grove surrounding the house were long rough tables and benches that had been prepared especially for this occasion. There was a huge outdoor fire-place or fire-kiln on which to cook the oysters and other sea foods.

The party, consisting of about twenty-five, arrived at the Point about two o'clock and found everything in readiness for the feast. And what a feast! The boys were tonging and bringing up great buckets of oysters ready to be put on the fire. Soon we had the entire fire-kiln covered with the finest oysters that Lynnhaven produces. The odor, like no other, began to permeate the air, giving every one the urge to eat. Each one waited on himself. We would go to the fireplace and get our supply and carry it to the tables where all the condiments were, exhaust that and go back again. There were steady streams coming and going from fireplace to tables all the afternoon. And in addition to this, the hostess had prepared long strips of tenderloin beef and brought along, just in case some one didn't like oysters so well. This tenderloin was put on long wire hooks and broiled over the fire to any consistency. You could have it rare, medium or well done.

The odor from the steaming oysters, and you know that is most delicious, mingled with the odor of the broiling tenderloin was so far-reaching that an airplane soaring above must have caught a whiff, for the pilot taxied right down, landing in the road beside the point. He came over and spent the rest of the afternoon feasting on the "likes of which he had never tasted before."

About six o'clock every one, declaring he had never had such a glorious

An Oyster Buy Boat, Hampton Roads, Virginia. Virginia State Library and Archives. [47917].

time, prepared to leave. We soon gathered up the things we were to carry back and with many regrets that we had to go, we were soon on our way.

The guests were invited to carry back as many oysters as they would like.[40]

∽ ∾

OF ALL THE FAMOUS VIRGINIA FOODS, THE EPICUREAN LOVES THE DELICATE, DELICIOUS CRUSTACEAN 'KING OYSTER' BEST

EVER SINCE THE settlers from "the old country" came to colonize Virginia in 1607, the oyster has been recognized as the most delicious and self-satisfying of all of the Tidewater's Famous Table Delicacies. And ever since the advent of Capt. John Smith and his party when they arrived at Kecoughtan (Hampton) and were entertained at an "oyster-roast" by the great Indian Chief "King Powhatan," it has been the custom of residents and organizations of the eastern shore of Virginia to enter-tain their guests in the fall and winter with an outdoor oyster-roast. Many a prominent and outstanding statesman from this and foreign countries has made visits to the Norfolk area for the purpose of enjoying a feast of this famous bivalve.

Virginians know what to eat and how to eat. Into the pages of many cook books have gone the receipts that have been handed down from generation to generation and even unto this day please the palates of those favored sons and daughters of the Old Dominion who live close to the waters.

But there are receipts that need the handiwork of cooks who know how to cook and oysters are prominent among the many.

We might add a good old fashioned Brunswick stew but that is a mat-ter not to be included in this article. It is worthy of a yarn all to itself.

There are many ways to cook the oyster but with the true sons and daughters of Virginia the roasted plate is the favored.

Good snappy weather, with a bit of chill in the air and a carpet of frost on the ground makes an ideal setting for the feast that is to come.

Usually the sheet iron lid of the well heated oven is ready when the

Picking Crab Meat, Hampton, Historic Peninsula, Hampton Roads,
Virginia. Virginia State Library and Archives. [47876].

guests arrive, the tables are set with their side dishes of crackers, ketchup, horse radish, celery, olives, pickles and steaming coffee.

To get the best results and quickest action, a couple of experienced Negroes are on the scene, armed with their shucking knives ready to delve into the bivalves and lay them steaming hot into the hot buttered plate. The oysters are heaped on the heated lid kept at a temperature that opens the shells within a very short space of time, leaving little for the shuckers to do.

The general aspect of an old fashioned oyster roast is one of great pleasantry and [merry]-making. It is not unusual to see some trim little woman, with the suspected appetite of a bird, get away with several dozen of the roasted bits of delicacy without batting an eye.

Of course there are those who prefer their oysters in stews, some fried, but those folks are not exactly what one would call welcome guests at an oyster roast.

Just a description of the oven which as far as the writer can learn has changed little in the last 300 years of life in Norfolk. It is made of brick, about three or four feet high, solid on three sides and open in the front, a gaping space to receive the wood logs that are thrown in to keep the fires aburning.

Over the space on the top the square of sheet iron is placed and on this lid is placed the shovel (scoop) full of oysters.

The honest to goodness lover of roasted oysters needs little else to eat when his appetite is set for a good round feed of Lynnhaven, Cherrystone or the other first class oysters found in abundance in and around this port of Norfolk.

To the Northerners, inexperienced in so much, and especially in the preparation of delicacies, don't try to hold a real oyster roast unless you have a son of old Virginia to supervise the work and at least one burly Negro to tell you how things should be run.

If you want seafood prepared in the proper manner and served as only Norfolk people know how, pay a visit to this Great Seaport on Hampton Roads.[41]

A FIFTEEN CENTS PIG FOOT SUPPER

A MONTH AGO gathered in the basement of one of our local churches, was a small band of Negro women consisting of nine in number. The president is an old lady of seventy years.

"Ladies, we's got to do somepin' to raise a little money. Les all put our heads together and think of a supper we might give."

One sister suggested pig feet.

Another protested. "Who wants ole pig feet? They give you indigestion. The last time the pig feet were cold and half done. Why can't we give a chicken supper like we did years back? We served brown fried chicken, potato salad, hot rolls, butter, hot chocolate, and every bit of food was sold."

"But chicken is too high. Les get back to pig feet," said the president.

"I cooked the last time and you all knows I don't know how," said sister Graham. "I had many complaints."

"Well I'se from Georgia, and everyone will want a second helpin' if you'll let me cook them," another member argued.

"All right. Two weeks from now I'll expect you sisters here at 1 P.M., and that will give us ample time to prepare our supper," said the president. "Let's divide our members and bring everything down to the knives and forks."

On September 29, 1941, the group gathered.

Sister Covington brought her pig feet—split lengthwise, put them in two huge pots filled with water. Into each pot she added a pinch of soda. Pig feet need lots of water and a tiny bit of soda. They let them boil until tender.

"Well I've collected a few chickens," said sister Curtis. "I make a savory chicken stew in the following manner. Brown a few sliced onions and a whole stalk of celery slightly in some butter. Add the chicken for just three minutes and then cover with water—just cover. Add salt and pepper, lots of pepper and simmer for an hour or until chicken is tender. Thicken the stew with a little flour."

On one side of the church kitchen, sister Jones was making sweet potato and apple pies. Such a good smell pervaded the atmosphere, the odors of cooking cabbage, chicken, pig feet, coffee boiling, and pies baking.

Came seven o'clock and the dining room table was laden with huge yellow brown sweet potato pies, luscious apple pies, bowls of potato salad, lavishly trimmed with pimento, green lettuce, pickles, mustard, hot chili peppers. On the stove the chicken stew, pig feet, cabbage and rice kept warm.

First customer was a fat old minister.

"Doctor said I wasn't to eat no sweets, 'cause I'm too fat— but bring me in a supper."

A beautifully arranged plate was taken consisting of a half pig foot, a generous serving of potato salad and lettuce and cabbage. Coffee and cocoa were five cents extra.

"Oh, dis sho is good food. Gimme another order," said Reverend Lee.

And so on through the evening, the pig feet disappeared. Only fifteen cents for a generous stewed chicken and rice or pig foot supper.

Some were taken out but most customers came in, sat down, and ordered a second helping.

And the small supper brought in seven dollars, which encouraged this group of women to give another in the near future.[42]

∾ ∾

FISH FRY

A FISH FRY is a community affair, held in a park-like place in the woods near a fish or mill pond or on the lawn of a plantation house situated not far from a fish pond or mill pond. Occasionally it is held on the bank of a river in which fish can be caught.

Committees are named in advance to do various things: procure a seine and superintend "hauling the seine," build with boards necessary tables, prepare material for out-door fires, clear the scene of the fish fry of brush and other debris, if held in the woods.

Fish are caught by "hauling a seine"—dragging a long wide net through the water. Usually men are employed and paid to do the hauling. The haulers—several at each end of the net—wade in the water while hauling the seine.

The fish caught are usually perch, bass, chub, and cat. Fish are cleaned on the spot and soaked in salt water immediately.

Primitive Clammer, Wachapreague, Accomac County, Virginia. Virginia State Library and Archives. [47928].

Fires are built between two logs placed six or eight inches apart. Twigs or other small material is used as fuel. Fish are fried in skillets or frying pans, so placed as to rest on both logs above the fire.

Usually a number of "black mammies" are on hand to do the cleaning and the frying.

Serving of fish begins as soon as the frying begins. Fish and other eats are served on temporary tables built of boards. Fish is usually served with cornbread—corn pone.

Quite frequently no fish are caught. In anticipation of such eventuality, each family always brings a basket of eatables: fried chicken, ham, deviled-eggs, pickle, pies, etc. So often a fish fry results in a basket picnic.

Folks amuse themselves in various ways: children play "tag," or "hide and seek," courting couples pair off and sit in shady spots or in automobiles (once in buggies or carriages), the married men assemble in groups and talk politics, the women talk and watch. Some of all ages play croquet.[43]

∽ ∾

A BIRD HUNT IN FRANKLIN COUNTY, VIRGINIA, THIRTY YEARS AGO

DR. _____ CAME IN one night from a late call and announced to his wife that he had invited five Northern friends to hunt partridges with him during the Christmas holidays. The Doctor was a famous shot, and birds in Franklin County were unusually plentiful that year.

The house was an old fashioned one, built by his grandfather, of brick manufactured by slaves on the place. The only heat was from wide open fireplaces, and the only water from the lattice enclosed well in the yard. The wife knew the guests, accustomed to modern comforts, would suffer from cold and inconvenience, but the husband knew that the birds they could carry home would be ample compensation.

The guests, a physician, a lawyer and his young son, a merchant, and a druggist, arrived on Christmas during a light fall of snow, and everything was propitious for the adventure. Great logs of hickory wood burned in the open fireplaces, and the welcome which the hunters received was as cheerful as the glow of the flames. Instead of the cocktails to which they were perhaps accustomed they were served toddies, made of ten year old brandy, served in Waterford glass tumblers of a variety now almost obsolete. When they had made themselves as presentable as the primitive means provided permitted they were invited down a flight of twisted stairs to a large room in the basement where supper was served. Many of the delicacies provided were those hitherto untested by the men who were from New York, New Jersey, and Massachusetts.

At the foot of the table was a huge baked ham which had been cured by the smoke of hickory chips, and cooked with the skill commended by Mrs. Tyree in her famous Virginia Cook Book. This was magically carved in slices so thin that each plate was returned for "More." Potatoes were creamed to a flakey lightness which only Aunt Viney, trained in the days of slavery, could achieve. Asparagus was baked with almonds, covered with a rich white dressing, and served piping hot. In front of each plate, bedded in crisp lettuce was chicken salad, carefully prepared and marinated by the practiced hands of the hostess. Hot "pocket-book" rolls were passed frequently during the meal and coffee was served from a Sheffield container, many years old, during the entire supper. Strawberry preserves of rare flavor, and clear green watermelon-rind pickle, were beautiful and palatable entrees.

The dessert for this satisfying collation was white fruit cake, Aunt Viney's specialty, always a part of the preparations for any festivity, and home made ice cream which evoked exclamations of enjoyment from everyone. This concoction was prepared with great care by the hostess. A chocolate stock was made into which whipped cream was stirred, and to this was added sherry wine in which raisins had been soaked. The mixture was frozen by the old process of turning a freezer in crushed ice and salt. The result was "Nectar fit for the gods." Although the service left something to be desired, the food was perfect.

The decorations for this table, besides the old clear white china, the cut glass, and silver of forgotten patterns was a huge basket of pine cones and branches, surrounded by candles which had been moulded in the pewter moulds inherited in the family.

Daily the hunters went forth guided by the wary Doctor, and nightly they returned to meals as delicious as the first, with great strings of partridges which were hung outside to freeze. At the end of the holidays each man had a collection of birds which he could hardly carry. It was in the days before the law intervened to protect the birds from such overwhelming slaughter, and the exhibition carried by these returning marauders was the envy of all other travellers.[44]

∽ ∾

PROTRACTED MEETING DINNER

HOW WELL CAN I remember, one bright sunny Sunday morning in July, when the hearts of the good old Christians had been revived from the thought that they were preparing for a good old fashioned meeting, and a big old fashioned dinner. That morning the preacher could not finish his sermon, because of the amens, and shouts. But when the collection was taken up, and the minister 'nounced the benediction, the sisters and brethren laid aside their religion for a while, and went out to spread the feast.

I can see those old sisters with their frills, and frocks floating in the air, as they lined up on each side of the table of a hundred yards long. You could hear them talking a mile away, as they reached down in their baskets between their feet, for the good old Virginia snaps, cooked with ham, and seasoned with pepper and salt. As they stood around preparing the table, one would say to the other, "hun your cake smell better than mine. Let me tase it. Child you got a cake. 'Mus Nancy dis er cake worked me hard enough."

"Look er here Susie, did you fry that chicken?" "Yes," said Mus Susie, "I got up dis morning before day and cooked that er chicken." "You got me bested."

As the guests would stand around talking, and the good ham and chicken odor begin to fill the air, somebody would walk up to the table, and say to the sisters, "How long before dinner, Good Day I am hungry."

Then some old mother, with her back inclined over the basket, "Children, let us hurry up, de people done got de sent in their nose of dis food and it has made dem hungry."

After all of the food is put on the table, it would almost start water to run from your mouth, to see the pies, cakes, snaps, beef, chicken, sweet potatoes, white potatoes, pickle, steaming rolls, milk and butter.

Then you would hear the sisters say, "Go tell the guests and minister to come, all things are ready." When all have assembled around the table, then the minister would grace the food.

Then the sisters start dishing out the food, putting it in paper plates. Piling up the plates with chicken, ham, white potatoes, cake, pie, snaps and beans.

Every one would move off to some place to sit, and with his hand or fingers he would dip in his plate and pick up a chicken leg, and draw it between his teeth. Such eating and telling jokes such as these:

> Once there was an old colored man, who had never seen an aeroplane, so for the first time he saw one flying. He watched it until it lit, he said I will go and see what is that thing, so he crept up on it, peeping, and the flyer was getting ready to go back, and saw the old man peeping. He said to him, come over and go up with me. The Old man said, I don't know boss, about dat, when that ting gets wa up in de air and git out of fix, you going to say, Get out Negro, and crank that ting.

Another minister would say, "Didn't you know Jesus died for you?" He replied, "I didn't know he was sick. Had I known it, I would have taken him some chicken soup."[45]

∽ ∾

A PROTRACTED MEETING DINNER

A PROTRACTED MEETING dinner as one that stands out most vividly in my mind took place at McKendree Methodist Church in King William County, one of the four churches my father served some ten years ago. This church derived its name from one of its most prominent bishops, the late Bishop William F. McKendree.

A meeting of this kind was a great occasion, and one which was looked forward to from one year to another.

The membership of this church was composed mostly of the agricultural type, sturdy farmers, healthy and happy looking and their wives and children equally so. These kind people put their whole soul into this meeting and proved successful in more than one way.

Delicious fried chicken came first on the menu. [It] was cooked to a rich golden brown which corresponded with the lovely coloring of the leaves that hung from overhead branches. It was also crisp, tender, and juicy, and when one tasted of this delicious chicken it was at once understood that it had been prepared by the best and most experienced of old Virginia cooks.

Next came the roast beef. This was put on a large platter and sliced. Around this platter were placed boiled potatoes, that had been dipped in the essence of the beef shortly before the meal. This dish was garnished with parsley.

Butterbeans were brought in quart jars as well as half pints, and when the meeting was held during the week the beans were placed in a container and strung over a fire and heated.

Whole tomatoes that had been canned by the cold process took their place among the other vegetables. These were taken from the jar, firm and whole as if they had been peeled a few minutes before the meal. They were put on a plate of crisp, tender lettuce leaves, ready to be served.

Rolls, tall and little ones called turnovers, and biscuits were on the bread program. In the pastry line were 5 layer cakes of caramel, chocolate, and coconut. These were sliced thick, and were very tempting.

There were pies of sweet potato, chocolate, lemon, and little tarts of the same kind.

Iced tea was made in huge crockery jars, and large pieces of ice were placed in these about a half an hour before the meal. Lemonade was served with the cake.

Last, but not least, comes mother's thermos bottle of hot steaming coffee for Dr. Booker, of which he was so fond. Dr. Booker was presiding elder of the Richmond district, and King William falling in that district.

Dr. Booker would say to my father, "Sister Staples never forgets to bring me a hot steaming cup of coffee, which makes me feel better already just by getting a whiff of it. I appreciate the kind spirit which prompted her to do so."[46]

THE HUNDREDTH ANNIVERSARY OF A BAPTIST CHURCH

THE HUNDREDTH anniversary of a Baptist Church in Piedmont Virginia was a historic occasion. The church, spacious with its new Sunday School rooms, gleamed white among the primeval oaks that stand scattered over the ample grounds. Shrubbery around the church repeated the green patterns. A serpentine red-brick wall, a replica of the famous structure at the University of Virginia, encloses the nearby cemetery. A bright August sun, and a clear blue sky perfected the picture. The church is located on the historic "Old Plank Road" that connected Orange and Fredericksburg. It was down this road that Lee marched his forces to the battles of the Wilderness and Chancellorsville. The historic highway, now concrete, was on that Sunday crowded with cars from far and near counties, and from Baltimore, Washington, and Richmond.

The hundredth anniversary of a Baptist Church in Piedmont Virginia was a historic event that brought together more than a thousand people for an old-fashioned all-day church service.

Adequate preparations were made. Long tables made of boards were put up between the primeval oaks scattered over the spacious church grounds. Two barrels of ice were provided.

The tables, spread with white linen cloths, literally groaned with food. Whole hams, cured and fresh, and decorated with spices were set out and carved. Huge dishes of crisp golden-brown fried chicken, large platters of cold roast beef, veal, and lamb were served. Flaky biscuits, buttered turnovers, bakers' bread, home-made loaf bread and savory salt risin' loaves were provided. Potato salad, sliced tomatoes, delicious corn pudding and succotash, and sweet and sour pickles of all kinds abounded.

Pies of all kinds added color and good cheer. Meringued chocolate, lemon, coconut, caramel, and butter scotch pies vied with stacks of apple, peach, and sweet-potato varieties and chess pies were tops.

But pies shared the honors with cakes of many kinds and varieties. Angel food, pound cake, apple, marble, tall stacks of layer cakes— chocolate, lemon, caramel; jelly, coconut, and gold and silver cakes were among those served. Iced tea and lemonade abounded.

The dinner hour was distinctly social. Friends and relatives who had not seen each other for years met, renewing old friendships and exchanging family news.

Every person present was asked to sign a "Guest Book" which is preserved with the church records.[47]

∽ ᖆ

A PRIMITIVE BAPTIST ASSOCIATION OF FIFTY YEARS AGO

IN THE CENTER of a forest of gigantic oak trees a space was cleared and rude seats of split logs were placed on stone supporters, while a pulpit of rustic design was erected near. Here all day meetings were held on Friday, Saturday, and Sunday in late August.

On the appointed time a circle of vehicles of unimagined and now forgotten patterns, interspersed with horses and mules, whose stampings and neighings punctuated the discourses of the "inglorious Miltons," and "guiltless Cromwells" who filled the silent woods, and the long day, with lurid prophesies or glorious promises retained in the Scriptures.

Wagons were the method of transportation most frequently used, although many came on horseback, some riding "double." A few carriages and buggies ventured the perilous roads, happily unknown to modern traffic.

Into the wagons were piled whole families. Grandmother, dressed usually in new calico of a subdued pattern in black or brown, a calico slat bonnet of the same material, and a quaint little cape around her throat. This was usually fastened by an antique cameo pin, or one containing the hair of some cherished ancestor (for, believe it or not, these remote inhabitants were often the descendants of royalty, and had names which have pointed morals and adorned tales on many pages of history). Her long skirts concealed her white home knit stockings, but her coarse shoes were many sizes smaller than those worn by the grandmas of today. Sometimes she wore mitts on her roughened hands, but they were more frequently bare and testified to the pioneer usage to which they had been subjected. Mother wore a dress of lawn in some flowered pattern, or it might be a made-over silk which had served as her "second day" dress when she was married. The daughter just entering her teens smiled in happy anticipation, and the bashful son in his first long trousers, and the stairsteps of younger children scarcely left room in the wagon for the huge hamper filled to overflowing with the homemade delicacies prepared so lavishly for the midday meal under the trees.

There was the great ham of the chocolate colored variety so dear to southern palates, a platter of chicken fried to so delicate a brown, and piled to such height, as cannot be described. A roast of beef sufficient for a regiment had been cut from the choicest part of the animal butchered by the farmer for this particular occasion. A stone jar of cucumber pickle, planted, tended, gathered, browned and treasured for this particular day, another of "sweetmeats," made from the rind of watermelons and carved in fancy figures added zest to the feast. A large box of tea cakes cut in heart and diamond shapes were eagerly sought by the young. The pound cake, necessity of every occasion of festivity, was present in two varieties. The one flavored with brandy was passed to the unregenerate, while the other was reserved for the clergy and his followers.

There were biscuits to accompany the meal. These were either made with soda and buttermilk, and constituted the soft variety sought by the toothless, or beaten biscuit which the energy of tireless housewives provided in the days when labor saving devices were unknown.

The preacher entered the pulpit, which was the forum of the times, at about ten in the morning and his eloquence echoed in the clearing for about two hours, when he was ready for the mid-day re-past. His discourse was interrupted with a singing of hymns. Since there was only one available hymn book, the clergyman read two lines of the selected hymn and the congregation sang these, after which he read the next two lines and continued in this manner to the end. The deep bass voices of the men mingled with the clear untrained sopranos of the women in a harmony which the wide outdoors softened pleasantly.

Dinner was served at twelve promptly, all visitors being invited to share in the bounty provided.

After the repast the congregation reassembled on the uncomfortable seats, listened to more discourses, and joined in singing the hymns which were again "lined out."

Every household, however small, had guests for the night, and each day's service was a repetition of the former day, but each day increased the size of the gathering, and each day the hampers of food grew larger, and the capacity of the homes was more taxed. This gathering was the event of each succeeding year, the one to which the whole community looked forward and for which they prepared months in advance.[48]

∽ ∾

FAMILY REUNION

THE JORDANS OF VIRGINIA were gathering—Jordans, if you please, and all descended from one Samuel, who came to Jamestown soon after the colony was founded in 1607. None remembers when these reunions began. At any rate, they have been better attended in recent years— what with good roads and automobiles and increased prosperity. Jordans, moreover, have married in many directions, and now they come bearing names of all sorts.

Indeed, Grandma Cecily spends much time deploring the intrusion of "foreigners" upon the sacred limbs of the family tree. For instance, there are the Savedges of the Eastern Shore, who proudly claim descent from the lad adopted by Debedeavon—the "Laughing King," the Bowmans of Northern Virginia—merges with the family of Joist Hite, that stalwart German who brought a flock of people from Pennsylvania to settle Frederick County; the Bufords of Brunswick, all most legally minded; the Stuarts of Southwest Virginia, who talk much of Scottish ancestors. There's scarcely a Tidewater family, moreover, that is not represented on some limb of the spreading tree. Grandma Cecily, one of the few remaining Jordans by birth, now bears the name of Jones.

"Tut, tut!" she always says. "Joneses are fine people—Welsh and of the royalty. My husband was ap-Catesby, meaning that his mother was a Catesby. Others are always 'ap something.' "

For decades Grandma Cecily has presided at Jordan reunions—a right no one would have the effrontery to contest, since she was named for a most alluring ancestress. The earlier Cecily— only 22 at the death of Samuel Jordan—engaged herself to "two several men at the same time," suffered suit for breach of promise, and heard herself reprimanded by the governor, though that was in 1623, Grandma is still remembering the pleasant publicity.

Now servants were spreading heavy white damask on long tables and lifting silver from great hampers.

"Hurry," Grandma directed as a car entered the horseshoe drive, "the foreigners are coming."

"What do you mean—foreigners?" asked a sixteen-year old, who fell upon the old lady. The girl's curls had a Nordic hue and r's twirled from the end of her tongue.

"I reckon I mean you," Grandma retorted. "But Anna Maria, your Hite ancestors have been in Virginia more than two hundred years; so you ought to be naturalized right soon."

"Yes, I know Granny, a hundred years behind the Jordans. But those Hite girls that married Bowmans handed down some spiffy recipes. We've brought swell food to the reunion. Don't you like"—"No, I don't," snapped Grandma, "if you mean sauerkraut or scrapple."

"But sweet dumplings—oozy sweet—to be heated in your kitchen." And in anticipation Anna Maria smacked her very red lips.

Other descendants were evacuating cars arriving now in gala procession. "Gracious me!" said Grandma Cecily, "the Bufords from Brunswick County. How those people do like to argue! They've probably brought some of that stew just to start conversation."

"Why shouldn't we like to argue?" asked a tall young man, who held a very pretty girl by the hand, "Bufords never lose a case. Here's Priscilla—my most recent evidence. Took a lot of forensics—but I won her."

The color mounted to Grandma's cheeks.

"Oh, I know you spoke for yourself, Ted. I do love brides, even when they come from Massachusetts colleges. That girl's school at Harvard finished you off, didn't it, dear?"

"No, I'm not that bad," the new bride laughed. "Wellesley did the work, and I don't even know whether Harvard or William and Mary was founded first."

"You'll do," said Grandma, "a New Englander who doesn't know everything!"

"Another foreigner," volunteered Anna Maria, "for Grandma to tell about Tidewater cooking."

"Well," said Grandma resignedly, "I suppose people do have to marry outside their families."

"And so you happened," Flora countered. "Jordans, Carters, Harrisons, Randolphs, good old Tories of the Established Church all mixed with Broadduses, Gaineses, Pendletons, and other rebels against everything established."

"But remember," said Grandma, "that I can't stand new-fangled food at family reunions. But child, look at the cars. How the clan has multiplied!"

"Too bad old Samuel Jordan can't be here to see the result of his labors," Ted Buford volunteered.

Grandma Jones' cheeks were flushed; and Grandpa Jones, as ruffled as an old turkey gobbler in a barnyard of mixed fowl, began his usual connubial admonitions.

"Calm yourself, Cecily," he said. "Remember your heart never has been good."

"Strong enough to cause you a deal of concern," his wife retorted. "Look, Nathaniel, the Stuarts from the Southwest. I wonder what kind of food they'll bring!"

By noon the old house—with its wide center hall and four big square rooms, upstairs and down was filled with roaming descendants and collaterals, and the lawn swarmed with Virginians in whose veins flowed blood of many origins. Boys and girls swam in the James or lay stretched upon the landing that once had welcomed ships from foreign ports; men threw horseshoes under ancient trees; and a carefully selected committee of women set food upon the long tables.

"Well, this is real fried chicken," Grandma remarked as she viewed platters piled high with their golden brown contents, "just dipped in flour and fried in deep fat."

"There you go being provincial," said the daughter who had married into Northern Virginia. "Maryland fried chicken is very good."

"What *is* the difference?" asked the Buford bride.

"Ours is just crisp on the outside," Ted explained. "The other is encased in concrete."

"Batter doesn't always turn into concrete," Grandma interposed generously, "but here are two very correct hams."

"Mine is peanut-fed—the real Smithfield variety," this from a resident of Isle of Wight County. "It was soaked over night, boiled 20 minutes to the pound, skinned, and baked slowly for an hour. No cracker crumbs and cloves and cherries and pineapple for decoration."

"Exactly," Grandma approved. "Why gild the lily? I used an old Virginia method for cooking mine—wrapped it in a thick blanket of dough, baked it slowly, skinned it, and put it back in the oven to bake again."

"Yum, yum," exulted a lad who just come up from the river dripping. "Gimme, gimme!"

"Run along," ordered Grandma, "we've no time now to bother with men."

The women were busy at that. One blended the ingredients of chicken salad, while another lifted mysterious viands from a basket. Anna Maria Bowman, standing on the sidelines, was still smacking her pretty lips.

"Isn't that barbecued lamb?" she asked.

"It is," replied one of her elders. "I cooked it myself out of doors."

"These clam fritters should be heated," said a Savedge relative from the Eastern Shore.

"Give them to Mammy Sarah," Grandma Cecily directed. "They look delicious."

"How are they made?" the Wellesley graduate inquired.

"By an old Eastern Shore method," was the reply. "Plenty of fat clams, chopped fine, seasoned highly, thickened with stiff batter, and fried in deep fat. I've brought a bird pie. Lots of birds stop with us in late August, you know. Since 1914 it's been against the law to shoot them."

"I see you have terrapins straight from the marsh," said Grandma. "Tell this Yankee child how to cook terrapins."

"Just throw them alive into boiling water and then pick out the black meat. Here's the wine sauce too."

"Everybody who brought vegetables, take them to the summer kitchen," Grandma ordered, nodding toward the old brick building beside the house. "The corn pudding is already in the oven."

"How do you make corn pudding?" inquired Priscilla from Massachusetts. Grandma was obliging.

"Two cups of whole kernels, three eggs, a tablespoon of sugar, and a pint of rich milk, an egg-size of butter, mixed and baked as you would a custard. And I might as well mention spoon bread if you want to make a Buford happy. Scald one cup of white cornmeal, add a pint of rich milk, cook the mush ten minutes. Add another pint of milk and a heaping tablespoon of shortening, cool, and add four beaten eggs and a heaping teaspoon of baking powder. Bake in a slow oven. When it's done, don't think it's a New England Johnny cake and try to cut it with a knife. Now where are the desserts?"

Immediately the delicacies emerged from many baskets.

"Cottage cheese pie," exclaimed a descendant from the Tidewater. "Who on earth thought that up?"

"Hush," said a representative of the Valley. "We foreigners bring the best pies."

"But what about chess pies?" asked a representative of the Tidewater.

"Chess pies—not cheese—are indigenous to Eastern Virginia," the young lawyer remarked pompously.

"What does indigenous mean?" asked Anna Maria.

"Look it up," said Grandma Cecily.

"She thought chess pie was a typographical error," rolled from the legal tongue.

"Tut, tut!" said Grandma. "Here's a chess pie worth writing about. Tell her how you made it, Betsy."

"Easy enough. Cream 12 egg yolks into three-fourths of a pound of butter and one pound of sugar, if you have first washed the salt out of the butter. Then pour into a very short pie crust and bake slowly."

"Yes," said Grandma, "and the filling is actually so clear you can see through it."

Then she changed the subject by injecting an inquiry that had to do with pound cake. The dessert, forthwith produced, was alleged to be a pound for pound creation. Certainly, no "sad streak" marred its homogeneity.

"When do we eat?" asked Anna Maria.

"Not until everybody has had a mint julep," Grandma replied. "These are being made just right. The children may drain the glasses."

"Do tell me just how a mint julep is made."

It was Priscilla who again rose to the occasion. Clearly she was making a great hit with Grandma.

"Of course, Nathaniel knows better, but since he's busy doing the work, I'll try to tell you. Nathaniel and Colonel Harrison never settled the argument, but each one managed to drink the other's juleps. Colonel Harrison always made a syrup and always bruised the mint. Nathaniel mixes a teaspoonful of sugar in two jiggers of whiskey and adds a jigger of brandy. He crushes his ice in a napkin. Of course, the ice mustn't be washed after it's crushed, if you want the goblet to frost. He puts three sprigs of mint in the goblet to tickle the nose of the drinker. Then he fills the goblet with ice and pours in the liquor. I will say that my Nathaniel can produce the finest coating of frost I've ever seen. On one point he and the Colonel agreed—the goblet had to be silver."

A small boy rounded the house.

"Ain't there gonna be any ice cream?" he panted.

"Of course!" Grandma said soothingly, "and made in a real freezer—rich cream and fresh peaches. And Mammy's cooking vegetables I haven't had time to tell you about—turnip greens, black-eyed peas, collards, and . . . "

"Bicarbonate of soda," added the young lawyer from Brunswick.

Nobody heard, however, for Grandpa Nathaniel Jones, a goblet in hand, was approaching unsteadily, followed by Uncle Ezra—the butler—and Mammy Sarah, each carrying a silver tray with its frosted burden shimmering beneath the noonday sun.

"You've been tasting again—sipping before and after pouring," said Grandma Cecily. "Not another drop for you!"

But this was Grandpa's day for independence. He escaped to the head of the long table and lifted his goblet high above the Virginia ham that awaited his carving skill. A few luscious slices—translucent amber fat and tender meat the color of brick dust—lay atop the crisp surface. Grandpa Nathaniel blinked as his misty eyes took in the scene before him—salads that were gold or red; platters of fried chicken that glowed like early twilight; pickles as green and tender as the first shoots of spring; pies that resembled floating clouds or autumnal leaves; steaming dishes of vegetables that had drawn their hues from the rainbow; biscuits, rolls, spoon bread—all dripping yellow butter. Grandpa blinked again, breathed deep, and raised his goblet still higher.

"Descendants of Samuel Jordan," he said in tones reminiscent of the Taylor, Broaddus, and Gaines ancestors, whose oratory had enthralled the multitudes, "I am privileged to be here because the beauteous Cecily gave me admittance into the Jordan family. The descendants of Samuel have come from the four corners of Virginia to honor illustrious ancestors and to pledge their allegiance to freedom—and good food. Drink to Virginia, my children."

"To America," quavered Grandma Cecily, "to the little newcomer whose ancestor may have been aboard the Mayflower—to the Scotch-Irish and Germans of the Valley, to the English, Welsh, French of Tidewater—Americans first but Virginians always."[49]

∾ ∾

THE WESTMORELAND PUBLIC EATS

BEING A MEMBER of the Stratford Committee has its advantages as well as its burdens, even though pleasant ones. For instance, a Westmoreland County member never has to pay an entrance fee, no matter what entertainment is being given at Stratford—but the Westmoreland Stratford Committee is on the spot when the question of entertaining the public comes up, whether it be to act as hostesses during garden week, or to provide amusement as well as food when the public is invited.

Every spring and fall the Directors of the Robert E. Lee Memorial Foundation come to Stratford for a week of business meetings, and on one of these occasions, late in the spring several years ago, word came that Mrs. Franklin Delano Roosevelt was coming to visit this shrine. Immediately the Westmoreland Committee offered to give a luncheon for her party on the grounds at Stratford.

As soon as word got around that such a distinguished visitor would be there, the committee knew there would be a large crowd of curious visitors who would be more interested in seeing the First Lady than in visiting Stratford, and that this crowd would expect something to eat. It was decided to have a seated table for the Roosevelt party, and the rest of the crowd would be fed in picnic style. All the housekeepers vied with each other to see which could produce the most attractive and appetizing dishes. Knowing the extravagant generosity of the ladies who were going to be hostesses of the day, no attempt at a restricted menu was made. There always has been enough, and the Committee knew that there would be an abundance this time. Just a few suggestions to sub-committees, and everything would be there in proper proportion. And, as it turned out, this worked beautifully. There were committees on meats; breads; tea and coffee; butter, pickles, and jellies; vegetables and salads; and on cakes, pies, and ice cream.

The President's Lady's table was loaded with such delicious food as never was seen before, and the same things appeared on the tables from which the general public was served. Beautiful thin slices of home-cured ham, fried and baked chickens and ducks, cold lamb and fried oysters, luscious creamy Irish potatoes and candied sweet potatoes, sweet corn on the ear and also in puddings, fruit salads, potato salad with sliced tomatoes and red and green peppers garnishing the platters.

When it came to bread—well, the Westmoreland women are noted for their beautiful risen bread, rolls in clover leaf and turnover style, potato rolls, and puffy hot biscuits. Several freezers of homemade ice cream (not frozen custard, but made of all pure cream) and the most heavenly cakes of every description were served as dessert. Two angelfood cakes, one iced in pale green and the other in pale pink, took Mrs. Roosevelt's eye and she made enthusiastic remarks about them, eating a slice from each, and saying she wished the White House chef could turn out such delectable results. Pies also were served—apple, caramel, chocolate, lemon, coconut, and custard pies, some with fluffy meringue, and some with criss-cross pastry over the top. Could anybody ask for more than a luncheon of this bountiful menu?

Sixth Street Market, Richmond, Virginia. WPA Photographer W. Lincoln Highton. Virginia State Library and Archives. [43486].

Some of the hostesses were so exhausted by their preparations that they were too tired to attend the luncheon, one of them jumping in a car and leaving for Washington just as the guest of honor was nearing Stratford.[50]

∽ ∼

FOURTH OF JULY CELEBRATION-1855

IT WAS IN THE YEAR 1855 on an early Wednesday morning (4th of July), and the little historic town of Fredericksburg, Virginia was filled with enthusiasm, in spite of the threatening clouds which indicated that rain might commence to fall at any time. This was the day which had been looked forward to for weeks when the "American Party" would observe the Ratification of the Philadelphia Platform.

People from all of the adjoining counties were here early, eager to participate in the parade. The "Banner Delegation" consisted of Staffordians (from Stafford) and the procession was one half a mile long.

By ten o'clock the city hall was filled to overflowing (many standing outside) with young girls and their sweethearts, newlyweds, older men and their wives, old men who had suffered many privations, hardships, and had so successfully helped make a fine country.

The Declaration was impressively read and received with a deafening applause. The band played well and impressively. It is estimated that between 1,500 to 2,500 attended this festive celebration. In two hours 140 badges were given out and not half received the much sought-for token.

The procession was headed by the Chariot of the Band, hung with festoons of flowers, adorned with wreaths of roses, and crowned and ornamented by thirteen little girls. Thirteen little beauties, each wearing a tiny flag of the "Stars and Stripes," the whole drawn by four well groomed white horses. It was a picture worthy to be called fairy land with a beautiful landscape.

The delegations endeavored to surpass [each other] in making their banners as artistic and appropriate as possible. Among them we read as follows:

Put None But Americans on Guard
The Bible and the Constitution
Our Country First, Our Country Last, Our Country Ever
The Stars and Stripes are Ours
Aliens May Ride In the Chariot of Freedom, but Americans
    Must Hold the Reins
Uncompromising Hostility to All Papal Influence
The Union, the Whole Union, and Nothing But the Union
Support American Measures
No Recantation to Make
Protection to All, Power to the American Born
Extinction of Political Romanism
Our Country and Our Country's Good

The principal banner was a young American holding aloft the Stars and Stripes. In the background, an American line of Battleships and Fort; Bay and Mountain; then in the clouds above, the motto: "Americans Shall Rule America," underneath: American Council No. 32. On the reverse side: "The Flag of Our Union." The stars for its friends and the stripes for its enemies. An American Eagle above supporting the whole with a cord and tassel passing through his beak.

The procession marched through all of the principal streets, and the windows were filled with bright, animated faces of the ladies waving their handkerchiefs. At the corner above the bridge the procession divided into two lines, through which the carriages were drawn. The marshals on their prancing steeds formed an avenue, near to the entrance to the bridge, through which the long line passed in one unbroken stream to the Island.

The clouds had looked threatening all day, and just at this time, the rain commenced to fall and umbrellas were very much in evidence, those without them were very soon soaked. The procession and the enthusiasm of the crowd was not lessened by the weather. After they reached the Island the Resolutions were read and ratified; the Philadelphia Platform was also read; and both were passed with a shout or applause.

A gentleman from Stafford County became very enthusiastic and exclaimed, "I am the strongest sort of a Democrat, but when I am wrong I don't go for party!" The applause was great. Many did not get into the real spirit of the occasion until the Platform was read.

It was indeed unfortunate after so much work and painstaking care that the dinner should have to be turned "a damp dinner" indeed. The rain got into the salt cellars, butter, cucumbers, corn bread, plates and dishes, saddles of mutton, delicious hams, roast pigs, etc. The food was dampened but not the ardor and spirits of the people. The appetizing food, the patriotism shown, and the procession could never be effaced from the memory of those who witnessed and participated in the celebration.

About 1,500 to 1,700 had indeed an unusual experience in being seated on very damp timber. Friends held umbrellas over each other while they ate, taking turns in umbrella holding, and the one standing by had the benefit of the rain drops dripping softly down their backs.

The following is the scant menu for the Dinner:

8	*Saddles Mutton*
16	*Fore Quarters Mutton*
20	*Roast Pigs*
32	*Quarters of Shoat*
8	*Shoat Hind Hashed and Stewed*
26	*Fore Quarters of Lamb*
20	*Hind Quarters of Lamb*
500	*Chickens*
16	*Quarters Veal*
4	*Veal Heads—Stewed (Wine Sauce)*
30	*Hams of Bacon*
20	*Pieces of Beef, 10 lbs. each*
750	*Loaves of Bread*
6	*lbs. of Black Pepper*
50	*lbs. Lard*
60	*lbs. Butter*
10	*Bushels Potatoes*
6	*Bushels Beets*
5	*Bushels Onions*

*Newport News, Virginia. September 1936. A market in the Negro section.
Farm Security Administration Photographer Paul Carter.
[LC-USF33-10164-M4].*

320	Heads of Cabbage
10	Gallons Vinegar
120	lbs. Crushed Sugar
1	Gallon Currant Jelly
5	lbs. Mustard
1	Gallon Sweet Oil
2	Boxes Lemons
150	Quarts Wine
40	Gallons Whiskey
14	Bottles Brown Stout
6,000	Feet of Lumber for the Tables
150	Negro Waiters
12	Cooks Employed—2 Days

Glass, Chinaware, Knives and Forks, Spoons, etc., for 1,300 persons to be seated.

After a much enjoyed dinner, in spite of the rather unaccomodating weather, everyone adjourned to the Court House. The band played "Hail Columbia." The President of the organization called for the words and they were sung with great fervor. Many speeches were made, which were received with great applause and apparent interest. Some of the Toasts, which were rather attractive are:

The day we celebrate—The courage and virtue of a few who made it memorable, but a multitude whom no tongue can number will keep it in remembrance. (Hail Columbia)

The Constitution of the United States—The Arch which binds with its strength and decorates with its beauty, the pillow of its republic. (Star Spangled Banner)

To Messrs. _____ of Richmond, Virginia who furnished the liquor for the celebration—Three Cheers for our generous brethren of the City of Richmond. Upright merchants, warm Friends, and True Americans. Though absent in the flesh they are present in the spirit.

After a happy, successful day, the celebration adjourned at 8 o'clock, and the county people hurried home in their wagons, carriages, and buggies, and many of the Fredericksburg people wended their way home slowly from an enjoyable but fatiguing day.[51]

∾ ∾

SOUTHERN THANKSGIVING DINNER

Setting: The home of the Murrays, Princess Anne County, Virginia. A typical colonial home surrounded by large shade trees. The Murrays are simple minded, comfort loving people, desiring only to serve God and their fellow man, having no great social aspirations.

Occasion: Thanksgiving dinner 1941, celebrating the home coming of James Murray (23) who is a young lieutenant in Uncle Sam's army, recently on maneuvers in Alabama.

Characters: Mother, Lucy Murray, (53) quiet, dignified, with slightly graying hair and wistful blue eyes.

Father, Dave Murray, (56) tall, broad shouldered, with mischievous black eyes and teasing manner.

Uncle John and Aunt Sarah, brother and sister-in-law to Mr. Murray.

Philip Butt and Catherine, his wife, who is the eldest child of the Murrays.

Brother Dave, (26) a struggling young lawyer and his wife, who was pretty Susan Shipp.

Mary Moseley, young James's best girl friend.

Rev. Mr. Rhodes, the minister, and his wife, who are old friends of the Murrays.

Liza, the black mammy, who has been with the Murrays since they married, and Mose, her husband, who always takes orders from Liza.

Honeysuckle, young granddaughter of Liza and Mose, whose services are required on special occasions.

Menu: Princess Anne turkey, stuffed with Lynnhaven oysters, giblet gravy; cranberry sauce; Virginia smoked ham from Dave Murray's own smokehouse; spiced beef, also prepared by the famous Murray recipe; collards; rutabagas; candied yams; creamed Irish potatoes, crisp stuffed celery; homemade sweet pickled beets; watermelon rind sweet pickle; Liza's famous hot biscuits; golden brown Virginia corn bread; hot coffee; Virginia fruit cake; and Liza's luscious pumpkin and mince pies.

Excitement reigns on the Murray plantation when the news of Mr. James' home-coming was received. Lucy Murray, calling Liza, begins a hasty enumeration of all his favorite eats. Besides the "fatted calf," a prize gobbler is selected for the feast.

Liza, "I jes knowed at gobbler done been struttin too high. I sho is glad dat fruit cake's done cooked an a mellowin. Mose, you lazy bones, you jes come right here now an no mo loafin caze tain't no time ter waste. I ain't ben dis happy since parson Jones baptize me in dat ribber. Honeysuckle, bress yor heart chile, you take more pains wid Mr. James room den yo ebber done afore. Den polish all de bes silver tell it hurt yor eyes ter see.

"Yes'm Miss Lucy, I knows jes how much spice Mr. James laks in his pumpkin pie. Dat I does. Didn't I make ginger bread for him afore he wuz old ernuff to go to Miss Brown's school. Dat baby. Bress his soul."

The aroma issuing forth from the Murray kitchen while Liza's feast is being prepared would tempt the appetite of a king. The table is spread with pure white linen. The gobbler, browned only as Liza knows how, is a suitable centerpiece, the ham, sliced wafer thin, the spiced beef perfect, in fact, Liza's dinner is a complete success. Mose, in high collar, white cap and apron, shuffles around clumsily, while Honeysuckle in best bib and tucker is assigned the care of little Katie Butt.[52]

∽ ∾

THE WAY THE PEOPLE OF GOURDVINE NEIGHBORHOOD USED TO SPEND CHRISTMAS

WHEN MISS CORRIE HILL was a young lady and lived at her country home, "Homeland" which was situated near Gourdvine Church and near what is now the post office of Homeland, Christmas was a round of gaiety. She says that for a week before Christmas, the women folks were busy in the kitchen, preparing good things to eat. Cakes of every kind were baked, the fruit cake having already been baked a long time before. Pig's foot jelly was prepared because Christmas would not be Christmas without the jelly. Miss Corrie says, in telling of it, "We always

killed hogs a week or so before Christmas. The feet were cooked
thoroughly, the water in which they were cooked drained off most carefully and set to get cold. When it cooled the grease, which was later
used as Neat's foot oil and had many purposes in and about the house,
would be all on top and the jelly firm and nice underneath. Then the
jelly was put on to cook with egg shells and other things, the egg shell
being to clarify it, and when it was nice and clear it was flavored,
generally with lemon, and poured into a large bowl to harden again.
And was it good!"

Another delicacy which Mrs. Hill always made was chicken salad.
Miss Corrie also told of the making of that and smacked her lips
reminiscently over it. Always her mother, she said, made a water bucket
full of it. She did not use just the white meat as so many did, but
cooked the chicken until it was falling off the bone. Then she took out
all the bones and chopped it fine. Not having celery, as many people
did not raise celery and it was impossible to get it in the market as
now, a large head of cabbage, very white cabbage, was chopped find
and used in the place of the celery.

Miss Corrie said that they never had a Christmas tree. They hung up
their stockings though when she was small, and if the children did not
go to bed early enough to suit old Santa, he would come up on the front
porch and blow a loud blast on a horn. That was the signal that all
children must go right straight to bed.

"We never had over a twenty-five cent toy," Miss Corrie said. "And
we were happy as could be with that. Generally for the girls it was a
doll and never a large one for it had to go in the top of the stocking.
We also had some candy in the stocking, all wrapped up in paper,
an orange down in the very toe, and Christmas was the only time we
ever had oranges, then there were nuts all wrapped up separately too
and cake."

After she became a young lady too large for toys, Christmas still was
very gay for all during the week nobody on the farms worked except
to see that the stock was fed and there was a party somewhere in the
neighborhood every night. And everybody went to each party.

"We played games at the parties," Miss Corrie explained. Such games as Stealing Partners, Grab, and King William. When we got tired we sat down and played something like Thimble and Consequences."

The refreshments generally consisted of several kinds of cake, frequently pound cake, made in the old fashioned way with a pound of everything, and jelly.

And then one night during Christmas week, they had what she called a "pound party." That was always held at the schoolhouse and everybody had to take a pound of something to eat, nuts, candy, raisins, and such things. The same games were played.

"And of course, we girls were always well chaperoned," Miss Corrie added.[53]

                       ∽ ∾

A CHRISTMAS DINNER IN SOUTHWEST VIRGINIA

IN VIRGINIA WE go home for Christmas. This means in my family, go to grandma's, and only sickness or death could keep any one of us away. By Christmas Eve the old home is full from top to bottom, a merry crowd, ranging in age from eighty-six year old grandfather, to the latest six months old great-grandson.

Aside from the bulging stocking, filled the night before by Santa Claus, and the fragrant cedar tree upon which we all hang our gifts, the high light of Christmas day is the noon dinner. Grandma's breakfasts are no light affairs, but a meal of fried ham and eggs, lye hominy, crusty egg-bread, hot biscuits and honey; yet it is served early, and we know to eat sparingly, and save room for turkey and fixins'.

The ceremony at the Christmas tree is held soon after this morning meal, and then things begin to hum in the kitchen. Everyone old enough is given a task. The boys gather chairs enough to seat the entire group—no "second tables" at grandma's for Christmas dinner—and the girls set the table. Year after year its arrangement is the same. Huge bowls of custard, rich with cream and eggs, and seasoned with nutmeg are placed near each end of the long table. This is circled about by the tumblers in which it is served. High old cakestands holding pound and fruit cakes flank these containers, and pickles, cranberry sauce, with apple, quince, and currant jellies form an outer ring around the whole.

Inside the kitchen Aunts Sissie, Bettie, and Margaret, all covered with big aprons, are carving turkeys, slicing ham, and creaming potatoes, under the watchful eye of grandma. Black Cele lifts steaming pans and waits upon the entire group. The turkeys are the piece de resistance. Great turkey hens—"gobblers are coarse with less white meat," says grandma. They were baked the day before, but today have been stuffed and carefully browned. This dressing is no modern oyster or chestnut filling, but an honest to goodness old Virginia concoction of wheat and corn breads coarsely crumbled, and seasoned with sage, celery, black pepper and a bit of onion. The whole then being dampened with rich broth and fragrant butter. Extra cakes of fluffy stuffing are baked, and these, together with the great bowls of gravy, heavy with giblets, assure a plenteous supply. Even to think of this makes my mouth water.

The ham, with its old Virginia flavor, and the candied yams, are a Christmas staple, and always covered dishes of snowy creamed potatoes, celery hearts, hot slaw, buttermilk biscuit and salt risen bread, such as Cele alone knows how to make, add to the meal. Now the carved turkeys are carried to the table, one place at each end, where grandpa and grandma will preside. Everything goes on the table except the hot biscuits, and the pies and coffee, for the serving of these, and the removal of the plates, is all Aunt Cele can manage alone, and "no bouncing up and down" is a rule.

When we gather round the table, grandpa raises his hand, and we bow our heads as he returns thanks. Then what a chattering of tongues, and clattering of knives and forks as the meal gets under way! At length the last hungry child relaxes, the table is cleared, and Aunt Cele serves the mince and custard pie. The custard and cake is served from the table, but there is little room left for the dessert. Uncle John loosens his belt under shelter of the cloth, and Cele brings a wet towel and begins to wipe off greasy little fingers. Grandma leans back, tired but happy, and announces: "Remember children, Aunt Cele must have some help with the dishes."[54]

COOKING FOR CHRISTMAS

When in late November, the clear crisp air of early morning is pungent with the smoke that circles up from nearly every farm yard, signifying that it is butchering time, then actually begins the first of the preparation for the Christmas feasting, for without the products of the hog the average county larder would be bare indeed.

As one of the early planters once said, they had to have the Negroes to grow the corn to fatten the hogs to feed the Negroes; so today much of the year's labor has, after all, revolved around the fulfillment that the fat carcasses hanging on the pole proclaim.

Seed time and harvest, and now butchering, for what would Christmas eating be without a huge ham and sausage, hung in cheesecloth bags or else fried and packed in jars, souse, made from the feet and jowl meat, seasoned well, with usually a little vinegar added? In some households the water in which the feet are cooked is canned and kept to use at Christmas time, when, flavored with homemade grape or blackberry wine, it makes a clear, delicately flavored jelly that quivers and shakes to the children's delight. Likewise is some of the liver pudding saved to add to the viands. A "pony-horse" as it is called in the mountains, is a mixture of hog's liver, often with part of the lungs added, seasoned with pepper and sage, thickened with white corn meal and baked. ["Pony-horse" is a variant of "ponhaws," from the German "Pfannhase" which means, literally, "pan rabbit." It is essentially the same as Philadelphia "scrapple."] Where there are such contrasts in the living standards as in rural Virginia, there is usually great diversity in the quality and variety of the foods served. But, regardless of whether it is in the humble home of a typical mountaineer, where the dinner may consist of jowl-meat and field cress, with the added extras of sweets and possibly a chicken, or the over-laden tables of the more prosperous, there is always the unbounded hospitality, that without pretence offers to strangers and kin alike the warmhearted welcome in keeping with the spirit of the season. Suppose we visit the Hereford home, a typical country home, surrounded by fertile acres. Ma Hereford has been busy for weeks preparing for the holidays, all the children with the exception of one son, who helps on the farm, are married and away from the old home, but Christmas will find them all gathered there, in time to help trim the tree for the numerous grandchildren. There will also be two maiden aunts and cousins, and always provision for the "stranger within the gate" whoever he may be.

The two big fruit cakes were made weeks ago, right after the butchering was finished. Over each was poured a cup of home-made wine. The cakes were then wrapped in paper and put away to 'ripen'. For several days preceeding Christmas Ma Hereford had Gracie, a young Negro girl, in to help. They had been busy in the kitchen trying to get all done so that on Christmas day there would be less actual cooking to do.

There is turkey to be dressed (or possibly a goose), the ham to boil and then to stick with cloves and bake, basting it with sweet cider and a little molasses. There are also chickens to be prepared, either for baking or frying—if the Fall hatch turned out well. Mince pies and lemon with a thick meringue, half a dozen cakes to be made, two five-decker coconut cakes and a jelly layer cake, as well as chocolate and a sort of glorified gingerbread that is so soft and delicate it fairly melts in the mouth, black walnut cookies, and plain sugar cookies for the little folk who will become satiated with the abundance of sweets, often too, a steamed plum pudding served with hard sauce, home-made coconut candy (even the small country stores carry coconuts at Christmas time, and there is many a sore finger from the endless grating).

All the preparation that can be made beforehand is a help, for there will be enough to do on Christmas morning, for besides roasting the turkey and cooking the chickens and perhaps a piece of chine meat [pork backbone] that has been saved since butchering time, there are sweet potatoes to candy, slaw to make, and also biscuits for even with the light bread made the day before—it would not be complete without the almost wafer-thin biscuits, piping hot. Usually there will be added tomatoes and corn, canned together, and maybe a corn pudding, from the corn that was canned during the summer, to add to the vegetable part of the menu. These, with "store goods"—grapes, nuts, and Christmas candy—will cheer the inner man, accompanied with eggnog and wine, usually homemade, for those who do not want anything as potent as the traditional Christmas drink.[55]

CHRISTMAS DINNER

SOME OF THE HAPPIEST memories of my life center around the Christmas dinner. At that time the family met together in a happy reunion.

The meal was started with some kind of cocktail—usually oyster or shrimp. Then the turkey—baked to a golden brown and stuffed with dressing seasoned with sage and onion, and rich brown gravy—appeared. By the turkey was placed a platter holding a Smithfield ham, that too baked to a luscious brown—with several pink slices cut and placed on top. The rest of the dinner consisted of scalloped oysters, a green vegetable, often spinach, garnished with hard boiled eggs, a casserole of macaroni, butter beans or green peas, a salad—either fresh fruit or vegetable— celery, cranberry sauce, pickle, hot rolls, and coffee.

After this was eaten, the table was cleared and the plum pudding, over which brandy had been poured, was placed before my mother. The lights were turned out, and a match was applied to the pudding. Seeing the brandy burn from a plum pudding adds a finishing touch to the festive air of Christmas. After the flames had burned out, the lights were turned on again and the pudding was served with generous helpings of hard sauce, flavored with rum.

After the table was cleared, and the nuts, sugar plums, sweets, and wine, which had been temptingly arrayed on the sideboard were placed before us.

My father, who was a clever wit, always told his brightest stories and added to the merriment of the party. The dinner lasted for several hours and when we finally left the depleted table, the short winter day was usually drawing to a close.[56]

༄ ༄

CHRISTMAS ON THE JEFFRIES FARM

PREPARATIONS FOR CHRISTMAS got off to a good early start on the Jeffries farm. It began by the time the men's part of hog killing was out of the way, and it began with hauling wood. For a long time before Christmas, the teams pulled load after load of long wood from the woods to the house. As it was hauled in it was cut into usable lengths, one length for the cook stove, and this must be split, one length for the heaters in the dining room and bedrooms and still another length for the fireplace in the living room. And always each length was stacked to itself, in high stacks that went as far up as it was safe to stack wood inside of the wood shed. When the men finished getting in the wood, there was enough and to spare to last all through Christmas week.

Inside the house, things were active too. Always, all the eggs that the hens could be persuaded to lay, were hoarded. And then the week before Christmas, Mother made a trip to town. She took the children with her and deposited them in the town's only ten cent store to spend their nickels and dimes which they had earned and hoarded all through the year. Such fun as it was, choosing things for every member of the family and the two grandmothers. The children came back in the buggy with many queer shaped packages which were mighty hard to keep wrapped up so others would not see their contents. But mother came back with big, brown, shiney coconuts, boxes of raisins and currants, cakes of chocolate and such things. Already there was a plentiful supply of sugar and flour which were always purchased by the barrel. And the baking started. Such sifting of flour, grating of coconut, greasing of cake pans, and mixing as went on. Always there was a sip of coconut milk for youngsters who were helpful, or a few raisins to munch.

All kinds of cakes were baked, chocolate, coconut, raisin, jelly, lemon layer cake, gold cake, silver cake, and always a big plain, pound cake. The fruit cake was already baked a month or so ago and along with the plum puddings which had already been boiled, were stored away to ripen. Pies filled the pantry shelves, mince pies, made of homemade mince meat made by Aunt Kitty Lewis's famous recipe, apple pies, lemon pies, coconut pies, and Tyler puddings which are pies too. Jars of doughnuts and cookies were also baked, the doughnuts being cake doughnuts dropped into deep fat and brought out just crunchy mouthfuls of deliciousness.

A ham was always cooked and ready too, as well as a big turkey which was never slaughtered until the day before Christmas. And woe betide the cook who did not know that turkeys should never be scalded to get the feathers off, but must be hung up and stuck through the roof of the mouth.

The children had their own part of the work to do besides just helping in the kitchen. It was their job to grate the coconut, pick out the walnut meats from walnuts which they had gathered themselves in the fall, and run the many errands that grown people cannot take the time for. When they became too obstreperous they were banished to the outside to bring in wood or something of that sort, and especially were they banished when the pound cake went into the oven, for that must never be shaken the least little bit until it was baked. But one job that especially belonged to the children was getting the running pine for the decorations. There was no holly on the place and very little mistletoe. But of running pine there was plenty. And they brought it in by the bagful, to drape over the pictures, door and window frames and mantel piece in the parlor. They never had a tree. They never missed it because, although they read stories of such things, none of their friends had trees and so they did not wish for one themselves.

And then, the much anticipated Christmas Eve night came along. It was very hard to keep little eyes shut long enough for sleep to come. Each child, before saying his prayers and being tucked between cold sheets in the nursery, had set his own chair where Santa would be sure to see it. Each of the younger children who still believed in Santa, had his own little chair. There was one which was a small rocking chair, one which had arms, and one which was a plain chair and was called "Little Higher" for no reason that any grown person could divine. The little rocking chair, the little arm chair and "Little Higher" were left side by side in front of the fireplace in a very conspicuous place.

And then, the next morning, such a shouting as each tried to "Christmas Gift" the other first. And such shining eyes as the children had when they found that Santa had left them each a toy, a doll, or a big story book or something equally interesting, an orange, some candy and some nuts, each in his own little chair. Breakfast was a mere waste of time but had to be gone through with. Candy and nuts had somewhat dulled the appetite for biscuits and home made sausage.

After breakfast, if the children could be held down that long, the members of the family exchanged their gifts which they had brought out from different hiding places. And then the trip to Grandma's house, quite close by, was started, each person carrying his own presents for Grandma and the cousins there. It was mighty hard to catch the cousins down there and say "Christmas Gift" to them before they said it to you. The house was approached with extreme caution but nearly always someone popped from behind the door and yelled "Christmas Gift" before you could do it to save your life.

Nothing dulled the appetite for dinner and the nice brown turkey which could be smelled cooking all during the morning [made] it seem as if dinner time would never come. And then, after dinner, that dull feeling that descended on little people so full of good things! A nice cold walk around to the rabbit gums out in the snowy fields, was a welcome change from playing and always brought back a feeling that supper of sandwiches and cake and this eaten in picnic style, would not be so bad after all.

No work was done on the farm during Christmas week. Mother did not have a great deal of cooking to do since she had done so much before Christmas. There was plenty of good sausage and liver pudding and such hog killing stuff for breakfasts, dinners were not hard to prepare from a well stocked cellar and so much pie and cake already cooked, and then suppers were just picnics. The men did not have to do anything except feed the stock and do the milking night and morning. The hired men had the whole week's vacation and went off to their own frolics. For the children it was a time for playing all day long. And for the grown ups it was a time of complete relaxation from work and worry.[57]

∽ ∾

HIGHWAY U. S. 1 IN VIRGINIA

EASTERN VIRGINIA, THROUGH which U.S. 1 passes, is the home of hot rolls and flaky biscuits; of spoon bread, batter bread, dodgers, pones, muffins, and batter cakes—all made of water-ground corn meal and rich with eggs and creamy milk; of Virginia hams, with amber fat and tender dark red meat; of Brunswick stew, cooked till the component parts are deliciously blended; of turnip greens boiled with Virginia-cured bacon and collards fried in bacon drippings; herring roe scrambled with eggs or rolled into cakes and fried golden brown and crisp at the edges; of chess pies and apple fritters, thick with candied syrup.

Perhaps in other sections of the country as good hot bread is made as in Eastern Virginia but never more of it. In the territory near U.S. 1 cold slices do not appear on tables. Three times a day two kinds of hot bread are served. Biscuits there may be or rolls or waffles or cakes made of wheat flour, but there will be also corn bread of some sort. The corn pone or dodger is still in good standing, and here and there will be found crackling bread and even the ash cake. An orthodox *corn pone* shows the imprint of the cook's fingers that moulded it into the proper elongated shape. It is made of meal, water, salt, and a bit of shortening and is cooked to a golden brown inside the oven. The dodger is the corn pone's closest of kin. It is fried, however, on an iron griddle. The *ash cake* is cooked in an open fire place, rolled in ashes near the smoldering coals. Sometimes it is wrapped in corn husks to save the trouble of dusting off ashes before serving. *Crackling bread* is the corn pone's richest relative, filled as it is with crisp bits of fat left from "trying out" lard. Spoon bread and batter bread rank at the very top of the social scale. The former is far too soft to be eaten with a fork. Its custard-like consistency is achieved by scalding the meal and sometimes by making it into a mush. To about one cup of the swollen meal are added two eggs, a teaspoon of baking powder, a tablespoon of shortening, and a pint of milk. Spoon bread is cooked in a slow oven. *Batter bread* contains less liquid, need not have the meal scalded, may be cooked more rapidly than spoon bread, and is stiff enough to be cut with a knife. By the way, no good Southerner tolerates either flour or sugar in corn bread.

Many *hams* that pass for the Virginian product, like young Lochinvar, came out of the west. The real thing is born and bred in the peanut section of Virginia, through which passes the southern part of U.S. 1. The meat is the color of Cuban mahogany, not an anemic pink, and the fat has the deep gold transparency of amber beads. Real Virginia ham is so tender that it can be cut by the dull edge of a fork. Contented hogs that have been fed on peanuts yield the delicious product. The smoking and the aging, however, are the second part of the secret.

Newport News, Virginia. March 1941. Men eating at the Salvation Army. Farm Security Administration Photographer John Vachon. [LC-USF34-62719-D].

Months of exposure to the smoke of hard woods and then other months of mellowing are necessary before a Virginian ham is ready for the epicure. Only a conscienceless dealer sells customers hams that are less than a year old.

Another much misunderstood Virginian dish is *Brunswick stew*. (Indeed, all that is stew is not Brunswick), and many a Virginian is thrown into a stew when he is subjected to heretical mixtures that foreigners try to pass for the real thing. The stew is a native of Brunswick County—and of course there is a story connected with its birth. Men, it is said, accustomed to bringing a variety of foods for hunting trips, left one of their numbers to do the cooking while they pursued game in territory nearby. The lazy fellow, whose talents were not culinary, dumped into one iron pot all the provisions, including the squirrels that had just been killed. So, a miracle was wrought.

Here is the way the ambrosian concoction is prepared. In 2 gallons of boiling water cook nine pounds of squirrels—or chickens, if squirrels are not in season—until the meat is tender. Throw in 6 pounds of tomatoes, 2 large onions, 2 pounds of cabbage, 5 large potatoes, 1 pound of butter beans, 6 slices of bacon, a pod of red pepper, and salt. Cook for about six hours. Then add 8 ears of corn sliced off the cob. Stir constantly for a few minutes and serve. This is the real Brunswick stew. Accept no substitutes.

As you travel down U.S. 1 you will be fed *turnip greens*—often called turnip salad or turnip sallet—and in season *collards* will appear on the table. No one should miss the *black-eyed pea cakes* that come in July and August. Turnip greens really should be cooked with hog jowl, the sort Virginian hogs yield. Now there's a dish for a hungry man, whether he has been plowing or working in an office, turnip greens and hog jowl—a food that should not be mentioned unless it is right beside you! If the jowl is not available, other fat meat is substituted in the boiling. Collards should be boiled first and then fried, for there is something indefinable about collards that requires the double process. In regard to black-eyed peas, the eternal question is whether to mash or not to mash, but along U.S. 1 in Virginia, the decision is usually rendered in favor of mashing. The peas are boiled with a bit of fat meat. Then

Sam Bens and Noah Booher, drivers for Associated Transport Company having dinner with a textile mill truck driver at a highway stop along US Highway Route No. 11 near Wytheville, Virginia. March 1943. Farm Security Administration Photographer John Vachon. [LC-USW3-20370-D].

they are converted into a paste, moulded into a loaf, covered with strips of bacon, and baked.

No continental continence that limits breakfasts to fruit juices and hard rolls or dry toast is tolerated along U.S. 1 in Virginia, for hearty folk, your hostess will tell you, should have hearty appetites early in the morning. Among all the many foods that are served for breakfast you will often find *fried herring or herring cakes*—whips for wayward appetites. The herring is rolled in corn meal and fried crisp. For the cakes herring flakes are mixed with eggs, and with potatoes, flour or corn meal.

Perhaps chess pie and fried apple pie will not be found in restaurants along the highway. No all-day picnic, however, is complete without them. *Chess pie* is made of butter, sugar, and eggs, poured uncooked into pastry and baked in a slow oven. *Fried apple pies* elsewhere are perhaps called tarts or fritters. Within their half-moon of very short pastry are sliced apples, mixed with sugar and spices. They are fried in deep fat.

If the tourist does not find Virginian foods along the highway, he should knock at some farmhouse door, register his complaint against American standardization, and be served after a manner that conforms to the ancient rules of hospitality.[58]

∽ ∾

HOW VIRGINIA SLAVES ATE

[ED. NOTE: The following information on slave foods was taken from interviews which were published in Perdue, et al, *Weevils in the Wheat*, which contains material from 157 ex-slaves who were interviewed by workers of the Virginia Writers' Project between 1936 and 1941.][59]

Mrs. Mary Wood (born 1858): Ain't Rhodie Johnson got dat? Use to come to see granny. Say on some of de plantations right in dat 'ar neighborhood ole marsters had troughs made—you know, like hog troughs. Would pour buttermilk in dis trough and crumble bread-cornbread 'course-in dis ole sour milk 'cause sometimes hit was 2 or 3 days ole. What did dey keer? Oyster shells was used to git up wid like you use spoons. Dat's end of dis tale.[60]

Newport News (Vicinity), Virginia. September 1936. Newport News homesteads, a U.S. Resettlement Administration housing project. Lunch hour. Farm Security Administration Photographer Paul Carter. [LC-USF33-10157-M4].

Uncle Bacchus White (born 1852): Dey uster to 'ave a big garden. I 'spose 'hit wus a acre and a half, uster to ra'se all kinds of vegetables. Colored people nuver did eat 'pargus and green peas 'till after de war, nuver liked dem. Dey uster to 'ave a big or'ard and I uster to steal the fruit. Dey uster to 'ave currants and gooseberries. Missie nuver lowed cab'age on herin table, she didn't like de smell of dem.

Dey uster to milk sixty or fifty gallons of milk a day. We alwa's had two 'omen to churn, an' dey wo'ld churn every day. Aunt Fanny uster to make us chil'en what we called "mush." Hit is made ert of corn meal. You take boiling water and pour 'hit o'er corn meal den let it git real cold an' cut 'hit ert in pieces, den cook it real brown on a griddle. Den aunt Fanny would put it in a large, wooden tray an' po'r milk o'er 'hit an' all de chil'en wo'ld git aro'nd and eat 'hit wid spoons which dey made ert of muscle shells. Dey wo'ld git these and make spoons ert of dem.[61]

Simon Stokes (born ca. 1839): In de fall wen de simmons wuz ripe, me and de odder boys sho 'had a big time possum huntin, we alls would git two or three a night; and we alls would put dem up and feed dem hoe-cake and simmons ter git dem nice and fat; den my mammy would roast dem wid sweet taters round them. Dey wuz sho' good, all roasted nice and brown wid de sweet taters in de graby.[62]

Mrs. Mary Satterfield (born 1861): She tell me dat po' nigger had to steal back dar in slav'y eben to git 'nuf t'eat. White fo'ks so mean didn't eben want nigger t'eat. Do nothin' but work day and night. Done heard her say she been in de field 'long side de fence many day an' git creasy [cress] an' poke sallet an' bile it 'dout a speck o' greese an' give it to us chillun 'cause de rashon de white fo'ks lounce out fo' de week done give out. She say sometime de men would go at night an' steal hog and sheep, burry de hair in a hole way yonder in de swamp sommers whar dey knowed de white fo'ks cudden fine it and cook an' eat it after us chillun was sleep. Dey waited till us chillun was sleep so dat ef de white fo'ks axe us 'bout it we wouldn't know nothin'. She say dey eben had to steal apples an' stuff lak dat as much as dey was on de place.[63]

Levi Pollard (born ca. 1850): Here de way us eat in slavery. Us eat breakfast 'roun eight o'clock. De folks dat was in de fields would cum home or else de ones at home would tote hit ter 'em. Dey go ter work 'round five en six o'clock. Dey ain't eat fo' dey go. Us eat mush en things like dat fo breakfast.

Dinner was half past twelve or one o'clock. Always nearly have boil dinner, er fried dinner er soup.

Fur supper most times molasses en bread (corn), er hind en milk, or suppers suppin like dat. Dis was 'round six o'clock.

After supper us ain't eat no mo 'til de next mornin' at breakfast.[64]

Horace Muse (born 1827): In dem days de only thing we got to eat was a ash cake an' half a herrin' an water. Ole woman brung us our dinnar to de fiel. She brung bread an' fish in a big basket an' a boy brung us water in a gourd. When I was at de Masons, dey feed us good. Dey give us a pint o' milk, a whole herrin' an' a ash cake too.[65]

Mrs. Sarah Wooden Johnson (born ca. 1858): Yes, I was big 'nough to see de Yankees come through here. I picked hard tacks off of de ground. We chillun would say to de soldiers, "Mr. gimme some bread. Mr. gimme some meat." Ha, ha, ha—and does you know dem soldiers jes would take dem ole hard biscuits and throw 'em at we chillun? I picked up a coat tale full. No honey, I ain't had no apron, ha, ha, ha—carried dem biscuits home and dropped dem in de pot of pot liquer dat was settin' down dar on de fir place kinder on de side. Muma had took all de cabbage out and was saving dat good and greasy liquer fer cush. Gal, does you know what cush is?

When in slavery time, you know, some time an ole slave mammy had lots of chillun to feed. De days dat deir mistress had bile vituals fer dinner you could have dat liquer and corn bread dat's left. Your mammy would crumble dis bread in dat good and greasy liquer, put a lot of black pepper in hit and let her steam a little while in dat ole big skillet. When she comes off fire all chillun gits a spoon and eat out dis skillet. Honey, dat stuff is good! Why er hit makes you lick your tongue out mo' dan once. We all chillun was crazy 'bout cush.

I done gone got off de track. We was talking 'bout dem biscuits, won't us? Well, dat day ain't had no cush 'cause my biscuits took up all de liquer gitting soft. My ant saw dese biscuits in de pot, say, "What you

Barbecue Cooking. Virginia State Library and Archives. [A9-14499].

put dem in dar for? Just like chillun—little dunces!'' Dat was right. 'Cause us was dunces. Ain't had no book learning like chillun now.[66]

Susan Jackson (born ?): At ten o'clock on work days dey would ring de bell an' dat was de sign fo' chillun to come fum de fiel'. Dey go back to de kitchen an' help Ant Hannah fix de food. She would take de cakes out, an' we would den put 'em aside to warm on a big tray. De cook fill- ed 'nother tray wid cabbage an' a bucket wid pot liquor. Den we take it all to de fiel', and de slaves lay down under a shade tree an' eat. Mos' times dey got half-hour, but nobody ain't gonna rush none. An' sometimes de ole overseer git impatient an' yell fo' de hands to come back to work fo' dey git done eatin'.[67]

Charles Grandy (born 1842): In de church de white folks was on one side an' de colored on de other. De preacher was a white man. He preach in a way lak, ''Bey yo' marser an' missus'' an' tell us don' steal f'om yo' marser an' missus. 'Cose we knowed it was wrong to steal, but de nig- gers had to steal to git somepin' to eat. I know I did. Dey had plenty o' food dere. Hawgs, cows chickens an' ev'thing was plentiful. Sometimes dey kill two an' three hundred hawgs but dey sell 'em. Didn' give me any. I got so hungry I stealed chickens off de roos'. Yessum, I did, chickens used roos' on de fense den, right out in de night. We would cook de chicken at night, eat him an' bu'n de feathers. Dat's what dey had dem ole paddyrollers fer. Dey come roun' an' search de qua'ters fer to see what you bin stealin'. We always had a trap in de floor fo' de do' to hide dese chickens in. Dis de way it go. Paddyrollers comin'! One come head ez a frien'. He let you know de other's comin'. Heah come de other bunch. Fust one say, ''Well Unc' John ain' got anything.'' Dey all pass on. Den he come back late, set at de table an' help you eat. He knowed you had to have somepin' to eat. So he'ud talk de res' by you an' come back an' help you eat it, dat's all.[68]

Baily Cunningham (born ca. 1838): We ate twice a day, about sunup and at sundown. All the work hands ate in the cabins and all the children took their cymblin [squash] soup bowl to the big kitchen and got it full of cabbage soup, then we were allowed to go [to] the table where the white folks ate and get the crumbs from the table. We sat on the ground around the quarters to eat with wooden spoons. Rations were given to the field hands every Monday morning. They would go to the smokehouse and the misses would give us some meal and meat in our sack. We were allowed to go to the garden or field and get cabbage, potatoes and corn or any other vegetables and cook in our shanties. We had plenty to eat. We had a large iron baker with a lid to bake bread and potatoes and a large iron kettle to boil things in. On Saturday morning we would go to the smokehouse and get some flour and a piece of meat with a bone so we could have a hoe-cake for dinner on Sunday. Sometimes we had plenty of milk and coffee.[69]

Lillian Clarke (born 1858): Ole An't Cinda say he [her master] and her mistress use to put one salt herrin' fish up on a shelf fer her to eat. Mind you, dats all day long. No, ain't give no bread wid hit. She had to eat dat or nothing.[70]

William Brooks (born 1860): Dey use to gib de slaves bout 6 pounds meat an' 5 pounds o'flour a week effen you ain' got chillun. If you got chillun, you git a little mo'. Well dat ain' 'nough lasten a dog a day. So dem niggers steal an' cose when dey steal dey git caught, an' when you git caught you git beat.[71]

Nannie Williams (born 1836): I was Ant Hannah's helper, and each mornin' mama would drap me past Ant Hannah's house. Guess dey was 'bout fo'teen chillun she had to look arter, all of 'em black babies. Deed, chile, you ain't gonna believe dis, but it's de gospel truf. Ant Hannah had a trough in her back yard—jus' like you put in a pig pen. Well, Ant Hannah would just po' dat trough full of milk an' drag dem chillum up on to it. Chillum slop up dat milk jus' like pigs.[72]

Aunt Susan Kelly (born ca. 1856): Mammy used ter bake ash cakes; dey wuz made wid meal, wid a little salt and mixed wid water; den mammy would rake up de ashes in de fire-place den she would make up de meal in round cakes, and put dem on de hot bricks ter bake; wen dey hed cooked roun'de edges, she would put ashes on de top ob dem, and wen dey wuz nice and brown she took dem out and washed dem off wid water.[73]

OLD DOMINION COOK BOOKS:
A BIBLIOGRAPHY

Bullock, Helen, ed. *Williamsburg Art of Cookery, or, Accomplished Gentle-woman's Companion*. Richmond, VA: August Dietz & Son, 1938. 276 pp., illus., bibl.

Based on, and as far as possible a reproduction of, *The Compleat Housewife, or Accomplish'd Gentlewoman's Companion*, printed in 1742 by William Parks in Williamsburg, Virginia.

Mrs. Bullock brought the earlier work up to date and consulted many old books on cookery—some printed in London, others in this country as early as 1812, and many of origin in this country, considered Virinian in their cookery traditions, published as late as the year 1922. The bibliography lists a number of manuscript cook books in the possession of persons in Virginia or nearby States and believed to date from the year 1801 to the year 1839.

Both as a cook book and a work of art, the volume is outstanding. In addition to the recipes, it contains "An Account of Virginia Hospitality; Treatises on the various Branches of Cookery; an account of Health Drinking; some Considerations on the Observation of Christmas in Virginia, with traditional Recipes for this Season; with the Author's Explanation of the Method of Collecting and Adapting these choice Recipes; and an alphabetical INDEX to the Whole."

The book is printed on especially made rag-content paper. "The Illustrations, by Elmo Jones, of Richmond, Virginia, are newly drawn in simulation of the Technique of the eighteenth Century Engravers and are reproduced with Line Cuts." "The Binding, hand-forwarded, by Meister and Smethie, of Richmond, Virginia, is styled on the simple Designs used by Parks on his less ambitious Productions."

Kimball, Marie. *Thomas Jefferson Cook Book*. Richmond, VA: Garrett & Massie—Publishers, 1939. 111 pp.

Under the heading, "The Epicure of Monticello," Mrs. Kimball presents an account of Jefferson's development from a rather provincial Virginian in the matter of cookery to what appears to have been a not uncommendable master of the "art." His may be designated the first modern American cook book.

"When Jefferson set sail for France in 1785, as Minister Plenipotentiary to the court of Louis XVI, he was, all unwittingly, leaving behind him the Virginia tradition of ham, fried chicken, Brunswick stew, greens and batter bread. * * * [sic] During the four years he lived in Paris,

Jefferson devoted himself to the intricacies of French cooking." The first American recipe for ice cream, then no vulgar commonplace, is in the writing of Thomas Jefferson. Most of the recipes are signed. Apparently Jefferson obtained them from friends and from the chefs he employed while in France, in Washington as President, and later at Monticello. The book reproduced is the one made by Virginia Randolph, Jefferson's fifth daughter, born in 1801, who married Nicholas P. Trist, later American envoy to Mexico. The recipes have been modernized to suit present-day conditions. Although not so extensive as the *Williamsburg Art of Cookery*, the book should prove useful to modern housewives.

Kimball, Marie. *The Martha Washington Cook Book*. New York: Coward-McCann, 1940. 204 pp., illus.

The book may be called "A Picture of the Old Virginia." In the "Acknowledgement," it is stated that the material has never before been published. A sketch of "The Mistress of Mount Vernon" covers some phases of the life of George and Martha Washington at Mount Vernon, New York, and Philadelphia. The inscription on the original reads:

"This book, written by Eleanor Parke Custis' great grand-mother, Mrs. John Custis, was given to her by her beloved Grandmama Martha Washington—formerly Mrs. Daniel Custis."

The volume is divided into "A Book of Cookery," of 206 recipes, and "A Book of Sweetmeats," of 326 pages. The pages are written in black ink, "in a bold angular hand." Inasmuch as Frances Parke was married in 1706, the recipes must date from early in the eighteenth century or before.

From a modern standpoint—aside from the differences in materials, leavening, shortening, and flavoring—the recipes appear to contain many omissions, especially the common articles of food, such as vegetables. They run largely to meats, fish, and fowl. Recipes have been modernized as to leavening and flavoring materials, and as to quantities used. As it stands, the book is excellent in the matter of the heavier foods, although it lacks the lighter touch of the latest cook books or even of the Jefferson book.

Smith, E. *The Compleat Housewife, or, accomplished Gentlewoman's Companion:* being a Collection of several Hundred of the most approved Recipes. Collected from the Fifth Edition. Williamsburg, VA: William Parks, 1742.

One copy of this work, stated as "the first American book on Cookery," out of but four extant, is owned by Colonial Williamsburg, Incorporated. It forms the basis of the present *Williamsburg Art of Cookery*.

[Glasse, Hannah.] *The Art of Cookery made plain and easy, by a Lady.* London, 1747.

A copy of this book is owned by Harvard University, Cambridge, Massachusetts.

The first American edition of this work was published in Alexandria, Virginia, in 1805. No copy of this can be located. "A New Edition, with Modern Improvement, Alexandria. Printed by Cotton and Stewart, 1812," 268 p., is in the Virginia State Library. The title reads: *The Art of Cookery, Made Plain and Easy;* "Excelling anything of the kind ever published by Mrs. Glasse." Containing "Directions how to market," and a long list of instructions of how to cook all sorts of dishes from roast to the art of preserving. "Also—The Order of A Bill of Fare for each Month, in the manner the dishes are to be placed upon the table; in the present taste."

In its day, it must have been unusually useful to housewives.

Directions for Cooking by Troops. "in camp and hospital." Prepared for the Army of Virginia and published by order of the Surgeon General with Essays on "Taking Food," and "What Food," by Florence Nightingale. Richmond, VA: J. W. Randolph, 1861. 35 pp.

The only copy available, a photostat, is in the Virginia State Library. The recipes run to soups and other hospital foods. It is interesting as a curiosity.

Randolph, Mary. *The Virginia Housewife: or Methodical Cook.* "Method is the Soul of Management." "Fourth Edition with Amendments and Additions." Washington, DC: P. Thompson, Way and Gideon, printers, 1830. 186 pp.

Also: a "Stereotype Edition, with Amendments and Additions." Baltimore: Plaskitt & Cugle, 1831.

An edition published by E. H. Butler & Co., Philadelphia, 1846, contains numerous manuscript additions. Another edition by E. H. Butler & Company, Philadelphia, appeared in 1855. The original copyright is to William B. Randolph, January 29, 1828.

An excellent cook book, comprehensive and practical. The recipes are not essentially Virginian. Its numerous republications indicate it must have been popular. Copies of all these editions are in the Virginia State Library.

[ED. NOTE. A recent undated reprint of the 1860 E.H. Butler edition has been published by Avenel Books by arrangement with the Valentine Museum, Richmond, Virginia. 180 pp.]

Harland, Marion. *Common Sense in the Household: a manual of practical housewifery.* New York: Charles Scribner's Sons, 1880. 529 pp.

A revision of the first cook book of Mary Virginia (Hawes) Terhune.
A first edition, published by Charles Scribner & Co., 1871, could not
be found. The work ran into various editions over a long term of years.
Copies of some of these later editions are in the Virginia State Library.

The book is especially interesting because of the personal touch. Mrs.
Terhune was born in Virginia, her grandfather [was] a planter of Henrico
County, near Richmond; and she was wife of a country parson of Charlotte
Court House. She explains that she put into the cook book much of her
experience as a housewife of moderate means in a small community.

Comprehensive and up-to-date for its time.

Harland, Marion. *House and Home, A Complete Housewife's Guide,* with
Original Engravings. Philadelphia: Clawson Brothers. Copyrighted by
Mary Virginia Terhune, 1889. 526 pp.

A book on manners and homemaking as well as cookery. Along many
lines, especially sanitation, the author anticipated by years practices that
are commonplace today.

Harland, Marion (Mrs. Mary Virginia (Hawes) Terhune). *Marion Harland's
Complete Cook Book. A Practical and Exhaustive Manual of Cooking
and Cookery and Housekeeping.* New Edition, Revised and Enlarged.
Indianapolis:Bobbs-Merrill Company. June, 1903; March, 1906. 728
pp.

The copy consulted, evidently not a first edition, is in the Virginia State
Library.

Mrs. Terhune's great work on cookery and homemaking was for years
the last word on those subjects for housewives all over America. Not
essentially Virginian, the book includes many dishes still popular in the
Old Dominion. With but little revising, it would be up-to-date now.

Harland, Marion. *The Story of Canning and Recipes.* National Canners'
Association. South Whitley, IN: Atoz Printing Company, 1910. 40 pp.,
illus.

The first known cook book devoted entirely to modern dishes from
preserved foods, it anticipates the era of the can-opener expert and is
still up-to-date.

Smith, Mary Stuart, comp. *Virginia Cookery Book.* New York: Harper &
Brothers, 1885. 350 pp.

"In the simplest and most unpretending manner, two Virginia ladies
would here-in lay before their sisters a collection of recipes such as have
been constantly used in the families of their State for many years back,
and tested by the experience of several generations."

An excellent collection of recipes for making good things to eat. Still useful if obtainable.

Virginia Cookery Book: Traditional Recipes, Richmond, VA: League of Woman Voters, Richmond, 1922.
A collection of typical Virginia cooking recipes. Copies available through the League.

The Kitchen Queen, dedicated to Rev. R. L. Mason, by the Ladies' Aid Society of Grace Episcopal Church, Richmond (now combined with Holy Trinity Church to form Grace and Holy Trinity). Richmond, VA: West, Johnston & Co., 1893. 70 pp.
A cook book of personal interest, the recipes signed, and modern in the sense that they cover up-to-date cooking. There are hints on house-cleaning and home remedies. Believed out of print, although doubtless many copies could be found in families whose traditions are of the 1890's.

Cook Book, Published by Woman's Christian Association, Richmond, VA: Walthall Bros, n.d. 50 pp. (Half of the book is devoted to advertisements.)
A cook book with the "home touch." General in recipes, not essentially Virginian. Modern [as] of date published. [Date not given.]

Menefee, Josephine T., comp. *Virginia Housekeepers' Guide.* "in Three Sections. Tested Virginia Recipes, Garden Flower Culture, Practical Home Suggestions." Roanoke, VA: Stone Printing and Manufacturing Company, 1935. 232 pp.
In the "Introduction," Blanche R. Davis, Past President, Garden Club of Virginia, comments:
"Your old Virginia Recipes are priceless. Many of them can be found in no other cookbook."
There are hints on table setting and service, centerpieces, seating, many pages of "sample menus," and—a modern touch—a table of weights of growing children, and reducing diets. Typical of Virginia; modern, but containing many of the "old Southern" dishes.

McPhail, Mrs. Clement Carrington. *The "F. F. V." Receipt Book.* Richmond: West, Johnston & Co., 1894. 266 pp.
In the preface Mrs. McPhail says, "Wishing to obtain the cordial and warm recommendation of my friends everywhere, I have endeavored to give only receipts which can be explicitly relied upon."
The contents cover not only the preparation of foods after the Virginia manner of the 1890's, but the cleaning of silver and brass, the washing

of dresses, and the polishing of furniture. Five "receipts" are devoted to the making of yeast. A thoroughgoing "home" cook book.

Moore, Carrie Picket. *The Way to the Heart, Hints to the Inexperienced.* "A collection of Tested Virginia Recipes." Richmond, VA: Whittet & Shepperson, 1905. 155 pp.

In the Preface Mrs. Moore says, "Having tried them, I feel justified in recommending them to the public as being safe and sure."

A cook book with the intimate touch, containing traditional southern dishes and many of the modern type.

Poindexter, Charlotte (Mason), comp. *Jane Hamilton's Recipes, Delicacies from the Old Dominion.* Chicago: A. C. McClurg, & Co., 1909. 190 pp.

Jane Hamilton was the wife of John Mayre, of Fredericksburg, Virginia, the youngest child of George Hamilton, of Forest Hill, the Hamilton home near Fredericksburg. It is stated, "The recipes contained in this little book have, up to the present time, never been in print." They were originally collected by Jane Hamilton's mother, and preserved in faded manuscript until they came into the possession of Mrs. Poindexter. The book thus "harks back" in the traditions of the days of Virginia's "old-time hospitality."

Pretlow, Mary D. *Old Southern Recipes.* New York: Robert McBride & Company, 1930. 211 pp.

"Many old and faded volumes," the Foreword states, "the recipes written in the handwriting of long ago, have been loaned me, and I have copied eagerly all those with the marginal note: 'still used in our family'. "

Though modern in style, the book speaks of old Virginia in its "hoe cake," "corn pone," "cornmeal batter cakes," "egg bread," "hominy corn bread," and other Southern favorites.

The Monticello Cook Book, sponsored by the University of Virginia Hospital League. Charlottesville, VA: The Michie Company, Printers, 1931. 93 pp.

An excellent cook book along modern lines, most of the recipes signed, the contributors covering a wide area, as Baltimore, West Virginia, Vermont. Comprehensive, including traditional old Virginia foods as well as many of the current period.

Famous Recipes from Old Virginia, by the Ginter Park Woman's Club, Richmond: Richmond Press, Inc. Printers, 1935. Illustrated by Margaret Dashiele. 224 pp.

Intriguing from such designations as "Amos' 'N' Andy's Favorite Dishes," "Cousin Jane's Almond Cake," and the like. Classifications are, (1) Early Virginians; (2) when the Club was formed; (3) from interesting People; (4) in Virginia today. A cook book of Richmond—and Virginians.

Cringan, Mrs. John W. *Instructions in Cooking with Selected Recipes.* Richmond: J. L. Hill Printing Company, 1895. 327 pp.

    Mrs. Cringan was teacher of cooking in the High School of Richmond,
Virginia; teacher of cooking in the Miller Manual Labor School of
Albemarle County, Virginia.

    A comprehensive cook book of general character. The recipes are not
strictly Southern.

The Farmville Herald Supplement Cook Book, (c. 1934). 75 pp.

    A sensible selection of cooking recipes—signed— recommended by
housewives of Farmville, Virginia and vicinity.

De Virginia Hambook by De Ol' Virginia Hamcook, "Recipes, Party Suggestions, Dances, Luncheon Parties, Menus, Philosophy." "Published at
the Request of Several Ladies." Richmond, VA: The Dietz Press,
Publishers, 1935. 50 pp.

    A strictly Virginia cook book, devoted to Smithfield ham.

Tyree, Marion Cabell, ed. *Housekeeping in Old Virginia.* "Containing Con-
tributions from two hundred and fifty of Virginia's noted Housewives,
distinguished for their skill in the culinary Art and other branches of
domestic Economy." Louisville, KY: John P. Morton & Company, 1890.
528 pp.

    A copy is owned by Miss Emma Lou Barlow, Williamsburg, with
manuscript notes added.

    A Virginia edition was published by J. W. Randolph and English, Rich-
mond, Virginia. 1878.

    Apparently this is a rare work. No copy can be located.

    [ED. NOTE: The original 1879 edition of this book has been reprinted
by Favorite Recipes, Press, Inc., Louisville, KY, 1965.]

Moeschler, Velna. *Virginia Cookery.* Roanoke, VA: Roanoke Printing Co., Inc.
1930. 120 pp.

    An excellent cook book of Southern recipes, still popular, contributed
by housewifes of the vicinity of the "upper Valley."

Church, Edith, and Bertina A. Leete. *Practical Patriotic Recipes.* Hampton,
VA: The Hampton Normal and Agricultural Institute (Colored), 1918.
16 pp.

    Edith Church was dietician, and Bertina A. Leete was in charge of
Domestic Science Department at Hampton. A modern book, the recipes
devoted almost entirely to "ration" foods.[74]

[ED. NOTE: One might also see Carson, Jane. *Colonial Virginia Cookery.*
Charlottesville: University Press of Virginia, 1968.]

Notes

1. Edward Arber, ed. *Travels and Works of Captain John Smith, President of Virginia and Admiral of New England, 1580-1631.* (A New Edition, with a Biographical and Critical Introduction, by A.G. Bradley). Edinburgh: John Grant, 1910. Pt. I and Pt. II.

2. Loc. LC/AE.

3. Written by VWP worker Henry I. Bowles, Richmond. Loc. LC/AE.

4. Collected by Lucille B. Jayne, Capahosic. Loc. UVA/FC.

5. Collected by Lucille B. Jayne, Capahosic. Loc. UVA/FC.

6. Collected by Lucille B. Jayne, Capahosic. Rec. 28 August 1939. Loc. UVA/FC.

7. No information on this item. Loc. UVA/FC.

8. Collected by Jean Deaton, Washington County. Loc. UVA/FC.

9. Collected by James Taylor Adams, Big Laurel, from Mrs. Mary Carter of Glamorgan, on 5 December 1940. Mrs. Carter heard it from her father and others ca. 1900. Loc. UVA/FC.

10. Collected by Cornelia E. Berry. Loc. UVA/FC.

11. Collected by James Taylor Adams, Big Laurel, from Patrick Henry Addington, "who said he had these "makin' outs" from his father, Thomas J. Addington and his mother, Jane Pirkey Addington about fifty years ago. P. H. Addington gave me these November 19, 1940, at his home on Rocky fork of Guests River three miles east of Big Laurel. Period was War Between the States, 1861-65." Loc. UVA/FC.

12. Collected by James Taylor Adams, Big Laurel, from Finley Adams, 2 January 1941. Finley learned it from his parents ca. 1900. Loc. UVA/FC.

13. Collected by James Taylor Adams, Big Laurel, from Winfred J. Kilgore of Big Laurel, 13 March 1941. Loc. UVA/FC.

14. Collected by Emory L. Hamilton, Wise, from himself, 3 January 1939. This item was intended for possible use in the "American Folk Stuff" publication. Loc. UVA/FC.

15. Collected by Pearl Morrissett, Danville, from Miss Martha Fuller, Danville, 21 February 1941. Loc. UVA/FC.

16. Collected by James Taylor Adams, Big Laurel, from Patrick Henry Addington of Big Laurel, 7 August 1941. Loc. UVA/FC.

17. Collected by Sue K. Gordon, Fredericksburg, 27 May 1939. Loc. UVA/FC.

18. Collected by Laura Virginia Hale, Front Royal from a Mrs. Grubbs, born near Rockland in Warren County in 1872. Material is from Mrs. Grubbs's grandmother, a Mrs. Stickley. Loc. UVA/FC.

19. Collected by Pearl Morrissett, Danville, from Della Barksdale, Danville, 7 October 1940. Loc. UVA/FC.

20. Collected by James Taylor Adams, Big Laurel, from Mrs. Mary Carter, Glamorgan, 8 April 1941. Adams says: "I believe [Mrs. Carter] to be the best informed person in this county on salit and salit pickings. Names and Terms are as used by her." Loc. UVA/FC.

21. Collected by James Taylor Adams, Big Laurel, from Finley Adams, 2 January 1941. Finley learned it from his mother, Nancy Ann Collins Adams, ca. 1906. Loc. UVA/FC.

22. Collected by Pearl Morrissett, Danville, from Miss Ida Stevens, Danville, 1 November 1940. Loc. UVA/FC.

23. Collected by Pearl Morrissett, Danville, from Amanda Stamps, Danville, 6 December 1940. Loc. UVA/FC.

24. Collected by Bessie A. Scales, Danville, from Mrs. Nancy Wooding, Danville, 30 June to 7 July 1941. Loc. UVA/FC.

25. Collected by James Taylor Adams, Big Laurel, from E.J. Bond, Big Laurel, 7 January 1941. Mr. Bond was born in 1861. Loc. UVA/FC.

26. Collected by James Taylor Adams, Big Laurel, from Mrs. Mary Carter, Glamorgan, 12 May 1941. Loc. UVA/FC.

27. Collected by James Taylor Adams, Big Laurel, from Leonard E. Carter, Glamorgan, who is a noted bee hunter, 18 June 1941. Loc. UVA/FC.

28. The time this event took place was ca. 1880. No other information available. Loc. UVA/FC.

29. Collected by Gertrude Blair, Roanoke, from Luther Trout (born 1868) and Mrs. Mary Poage (born 1858), both of Roanoke, 19 October 1936. Loc. UVA/FC.

30. Collected by James Taylor Adams, Big Laurel, from Elbert J. Bond, Big Laurel, 7 January 1941. Loc. UVA/FC.

31. Written by VWP worker J. Luther Kibler, Richmond. Loc. LC/AE.

32. Written by VWP worker Grant Jennings Smith, Richmond. Loc. LC/AE.

33. This material is taken from a longer piece entitled "Corn Shucking Time in Old Virginia," written by Gertrude Blair, Roanoke, from information obtained in interviews with several people. Loc. UVA/FC.

34. Written by VWP worker James B. Cook, Richmond. Loc. LC/AE.

35. Gay Neale, *Brunswick County, Virginia: 1720-1975*. The Brunswick County Bicentennial Committee, 1976. pp. 154-156.

36. *The Washington Post*, 23 February 1988. pp. B-1-2.

37. Written by VWP worker John W. Thomas, Richmond [a note indicates: "Negro man who is a Baptist preacher"]. Loc. LC/AE.

38. Copied by VWP worker Sue K. Gordon, Fredericksburg, "from an old scrap book," 7 June 1939. Loc. UVA/FC.

39. Written by VWP worker Alanson Crosby, Richmond. Loc. LC/AE.

40. Written by VWP worker Lelia L. McIntosh. Loc. LC/AE.

41. Written by VWP worker John E. Doar, Norfolk, 16 October 1941. Loc. LC/AE.

42. Written by VWP worker Louise B. Gow, Richmond. Loc. LC/AE.

43. Written by VWP worker H. Ragland Eubank, Richmond. Loc. LC/AE.

44. Written by VWP worker Essie W. Smith, Rocky Mount. Loc. LC/AE.

45. Written by VWP worker Isaiah Volley, Lynchburg. Rec. 18 October 1941. Loc. UVA/FC.

46. Written by VWP worker Gwendolyn Staples. Loc. LC/AE.

47. Written by VWP worker Meriam M. Sizer, Richmond. Loc. LC/AE.

48. Written by VWP worker Essie W. Smith, Rocky Mount. Loc. LC/AE.

49. Written by VWP State Supervisor Eudora Ramsay Richardson, Richmond. Loc. LC/AE.

50. Written by VWP worker Helen C. Tayloe, Richmond. Loc. LC/AE.

51. Sent in by Sue K. Gordon, Fredericksburg, 27 June 1939. The source is not indicated but was most likely the local newspaper. Loc. UVA/FC.

52. Written by VWP worker Sarah W. Moore, Portsmouth. Loc. LC/AE.

53. Collected by Margaret Jeffries, Culpeper, from Miss Corrie Hill, Culpeper, 29 November 1940. Loc. LC/AE.

54. Written by VWP worker Anne L. Worrell, Roanoke, 16 October 1941. Loc. LC/AE.

55. Written by VWP worker Susan R. Morton, Haymarket. Loc. LC/AE.

56. Written by VWP worker Elizabeth M. Nicholas, Richmond. Loc. LC/AE.

57. Collected by Margaret Jeffries, Culpeper, from Mrs. Maggie E. Jeffries [her mother] of Culpeper, 6 December 1940. The narrator here is Margaret Jeffries, not her mother, and the material presented has to do with Margaret's childhood. Loc. UVA/FC.

58. Apparently written 16 August 1937 by VWP State Supervisor Eudora Ramsay Richardson for the American Guide Series publication, *U.S. One: Maine to Florida.* New York: Modern Age Books, Inc., 1938. The only information on Virginia foods was a brief list of eleven items. Loc. LC/AE.

59. See Charles L. Perdue, Jr., Thomas E. Barden, and Robert K. Phillips. *Weevils in the Wheat: Interviews with Virginia Ex-Slaves.* Bloomington: Indiana University Press, 1980. Reprinted in paperback by University Press of Virginia, 1992.

60. Loc. HU/REL.

61. Loc. UVA/FC.

62. Loc. UVA/FC.

63. Loc. UVA/FC.

64. Loc. UVA/FC.

65. Loc. HU/REL.

66. Loc. HU/REL.

67. Loc. in Manuscripts Division, Special Collections Department, Alderman Library, University of Virginia. Found in draft no. 2 of *The Negro in Virginia*, Chap. 6, p. 9.

68. Loc. VSA.

69. Loc. UVA/FC.

70. Loc. HU/REL.

71. Loc. VSA.

72. Loc. *The Negro in Virginia.* Compiled by Workers of the Writers' Program of the Work Projects Administration in the State of Virginia. New York: Hastings House, 1940. Reprint by Arno Press, New York, 1969, p. 73.

73. Loc. UVA/FC.

74. The bibliography of cookbooks was compiled by VWP worker Henry I. Bowles, Richmond. Loc. LC/AE.

Appendix: VWP Writers and Researchers

[All of the following individuals are white with the exceptions of John W. Thomas and Isaiah Volley who are black; the race of Louise B. Gow is unknown. All cities and counties are in Virginia.]

Adams, James Taylor: (1892-1954); native of Wise County and a field worker there. Adams, with Emory Hamilton (listed below) is responsible for nearly half of the folklore collected by VWP workers in the State; also worked for the VHI.

Berry, Cornelia E.: a field worker in Northumberland County.

Blair, Gertrude: (1871-1945); a field worker in Roanoke.

Bowles, Henry I.: a research assistant in the VWP office in Richmond.

Cook, James B.: an editor in the VWP office in Richmond.

Crosby, Alanson: a researcher in the VWP office in Richmond.

Deaton, Jean: a field worker in Washington County.

Doar, John E.: worked in Norfolk; no other information available.

Eubank, H. Ragland: an editor and writer in the VWP office in Richmond.

Gordon, Sue K.: (1893-1971); a field worker in Fredericksburg; also worked for the VHI.

Gow, Louise B.: a worker in the VWP office in Richmond.

Hamilton, Emory L.: (1913-1991); a native of Wise County and field worker there (see note for Adams).

Jayne, Lucille B.: (1877-1945); a field worker in Gloucester County.

Jeffries, Margaret: (1899-1979); a field worker in Culpeper; also worked for the VHI.

Kibler, J. Luther: a researcher and writer in the VWP office in Ricmmond.

McIntosh, Lelia L.: no information.

Moore, Sarah W.: a field worker in Portsmouth.

Morrissett, Pearl: (1879-1967); a field worker in Danville.

Morton, Susan R.: a field worker in Loudoun County; also worked for the VHI.

Nicholas, Elizabeth M.: worked in the VWP office in Richmond.

Richardson, Eudora Ramsay: (1891-1973); State Director of the VWP, Richmond.

Scales, Bessie A.: (?-ca. 1964); a field worker in Danville.

Sizer, Miriam M.: (1883-1948); Folklore Consultant for the VWP, Richmond.

Smith, Grant Jennings: researcher and writer in the VWP office in Richmond; wrote numerous radio plays.

Smith, Essie W.: (1872-1963); a field worker in Franklin County; also worked for the VHI.

Staples, Gwendolyn: no information.

Tayloe, Helen C.: an editor in the VWP office in Richmond.

Thomas, John W.: worked in the VWP office in Richmond.

Volley, Isaiah: (?-1956); a field worker in Lynchburg.

Worrell, Anne L.: a field worker, writer, and researcher in Roanoke.